TYPOLOGIE DES SOURCES
DU MOYEN ÂGE OCCIDENTAL

DIRECTEUR : R. NOËL

LOCAL AND REGIONAL CHRONICLES

UNIVERSITÉ CATHOLIQUE DE LOUVAIN

INSTITUT D'ÉTUDES MÉDIÉVALES

Collège Érasme
Place Blaise Pascal, 1
1348 LOUVAIN-LA-NEUVE (Belgique)

Le texte de ce fascicule a été soumis à un comité de lecture composé de Messieurs Bernard Guenée et K.F. Werner , Membres de l'Institut de France, et de MM. L. Genicot (†) et R. Bultot, Professeurs émérites de l'Université catholique de Louvain.

TYPOLOGIE DES SOURCES
DU MOYEN ÂGE OCCIDENTAL

FONDATEUR : L. GENICOT
DIRECTEUR : R. NOËL

Fasc. 74

LOCAL AND REGIONAL CHRONICLES

BY

ELISABETH M.C. VAN HOUTS
Fellow and Lecturer in History
Newnham College Cambridge

BREPOLS
TURNHOUT-BELGIUM

1995

TABLE OF CONTENTS

PREFACE

The subject of local and regional chronicles between 500 AD and 1500 AD is a vast one, and no account of it could be comprehensive. This one is merely an introduction to the genre. Like other genres it is not altogether easy to define, and the definitions I offer in Chapter 1, together with my choice of illustrative material in later chapters, may prove to be controversial. I ask critical readers to bear in mind the limitations imposed upon me by the series; I have been anxious to avoid overlap with other volumes in it.

I have benefited greatly, while writing the book, from the critical comments offered by members of the Comité des Lecteurs, Professor L. Genicot (†), Professor R. Bultot, Professor B. Guenée and Professor K.F. Werner. I have not felt able to respond to all their suggestions, but they helped me to clarify my objectives and I am grateful to them. I am also very grateful to Dr Antonia Gransden, who kindly read the first draft and put me right on many points of detail.

Cambridge, November 1992

BIBLIOGRAPHY

Abbreviations

CDS: Die Chroniken der deutschen Städte von 14. bis in 16. Jahrhundert, ed. Historische Kommission bei der Bayerischen Akademie der Wissenschaften, Leipzig, 1862 - ...

RS: Rolls Series.

BAUTIER, R.-H., *L'historiographie en France aux Xe et XIe siècles (France du Nord et de l' Est)*, in *La Storiografia altomedievale*, Spoleto, 1970, vol. 2, p. 793-850 (Settimane di studio del Centro italiano di studi sull'alto medioevo, 17).

BODMER, J.P., *Chroniken und Chronisten im Spätmittelalter*, Bern, 1976 (Monographien zur Schweizer Geschichte herausgegeben von der allgemeinen Geschichtforschenden Gesellschaft der Schweiz, 10).

BOULAY, F.R.H. du, *The German town chronicles*, in *The writing of history in the Middle Ages. Essays presented to Richard William SOUTHERN*, ed. DAVIS, R.H.C. , and WALLACE-HADRILL, J.M., Oxford, 1981, p. 445-69.

CAENEGEM, R.C. van, *Guide to the sources of medieval history,* Amsterdam, 1978 (Europe in the Middle Ages. Selected studies, 2).

COCHRANE, E., *Historians and historiography in the Italian Renaissance,* Chicago, 1981.

DIAZ y DIAZ, M.C., *Index scriptorum Latinorum medii aevi Hispanorum,* 2 vol., Salamanca, 1958-9.

DIAZ Y DIAZ, M.C., *La historiografia hispana desde la invasion arabe hasta el año 1000,* in *La Storiografia* ..., p. 313-43.

DUNBABIN J., *Discovering a past for the french aristocracy,* in *The perception of the past in twelfth-century Europe,* ed. MAGDALINO, P., London, 1992, p. 1-14.

GANSHOF F.L., *L'historiographie dans la monarchie franque sous les mérovingiens et les carolingiens,* in *La Storiografia*..., p. 631-85.

GENET J.P., *Cartulaires, registres et histoire: l'exemple anglais,* in *Le métier d'historien au Moyen Âge. Études sur l'historiographie médiévale*, éd. B. GUENÉE, Paris, 1977, p. 95-138.

GENET, J.P. (ed.), *L'historiographie médiévale en Europe. Actes du Col-*

loque organisé par la Fondation Européenne de la Science au Centre de Recherches Historiques et Juridiques de l'Université Paris I du 29 mars au 1er Avril 1989, Paris, 1991.

GENICOT, L., *Les généalogies,* Turnhout, 1975 et mise à jour 1985 (Typologie des sources du moyen âge occidental, 15)

GOETZ, H.W., *Zum Geschichtsbewusstsein in der alemannisch-schweizerischen Klosterchronistik des hohen Mittelalters (11.-13. Jahrhundert)*, in *Deutsches Archiv,* 44 (1988), p. 455-88.

GRANSDEN, A., *Historical writing in England*, 2 vol., London, 1974, 1982.

GRANSDEN, A., *The chronicles of medieval England and Scotland*, in *Journal of Medieval History*, 16 (1990), p. 129-50; 17 (1991), p. 217-43.

GREEN, L., *Chronicle into history. An essay on the interpretation of history in Florentine fourteenth-century chronicles*, Cambridge, 1972.

GRUNDMANN, H., *Geschichtsschreibung im Mittelalter. Gattungen-Epochen-Eigenart.,* Göttingen, 1965.

GUENÉE, B., *Histoires, annales, chroniques. Essai sur les genres historiques au Moyen Âge,* in *Annales ESC*, 28 (1973), p. 997-1016.

GUENÉE, B., *Histoire et culture historique dans l'Occident médiéval,* Paris, 2e éd. 1991.

HAUCK K., *The literature of house and kindred associated with medieval noble families, illustrated from eleventh and twelfth-century satires on the nobility*, in *The medieval nobility,* ed. REUTER, T., Amsterdam, 1979, p. 61-85.

HAY, D., *History and historians in France and England during the fifteenth century*, in *Bulletin of the Institute of Historical Research*, 35 (1962), p. 111-27.

HAY, D., *Annalists and historians. Western historiography from the eighth to the eighteenth centuries*, London, 1977.

HILLGARTH, J.N., *Historiography in Visigothic Spain*, in *La Storiografia...*, p. 261-311.

HOFMANN, H., *Artikulationsformen historischen Wissens in der lateinsischen Historiographie des hohen und späten Mittelalters,* in *La littérature historiographique des origines à 1500*, ed. GUMBRECHT H.U., LINK-HEER, U., SPANGENBERG, P.M., Heidelberg, 1987 (Grundriss der romanischen Literaturen des Mittelalters), vol. XI/1, t. 1.2, p. 367-687.

HOUTS, E.M.C. van, *Gesta Normannorum Ducum. Een studie over de handschriften, de tekst, het geschiedwerk en het genre,* Groningen, 1982.

JONES, C.W., *Saints' lives and chronicles in early England,* Ithaca, 1947.

KASTNER, J., *Historiae fundationum monasterium. Frühformen monastischer Institutionsgeschichtsschreibung im Mittelalter,* Munich, 1974 (Münchener Beiträge zur Mediävistik und Renaissance Forschung, 18).

KRÜGER, K.H., *Die Universalchroniken*, Turnhout, 1976 (Typologie des sources du moyen âge occidental, 16).

LINEHAN, P., *History and the historians of Spain*, Oxford, 1993.

McCORMICK, M., *Les annales du haut Moyen Âge,*Turnhout, 1975 (Typologie des sources du moyen âge occidental, 14).

McGUIRE, M.R.P., *Annals and chronicles*, in *New Catholic Encyclopedia*, New York, 1967, t. 1, p. 551-6.

MOEGLIN, J.M., *Les ancêtres du prince. Propagande politique et naissance d'une histoire nationale en Bavière au Moyen Âge (1180-1500),* Genève, 1985.

MOEGLIN, J.M., *Dynastische Bewusstsein und Geschichtsschreibung. Zum Selbstverständnis der Wittelsbacher, Habsburger und Hohenzollern im Spätmittelalter,* in *Historische Zeitschrift,* 256 (1993), p. 593-653.

PATZE, H., *Adel und Stifterchronik. Frühformen territorialer Geschichtsschreibung im hochmittelalterlichen Reich,* in *Blätter für deutsche Landesgeschichte,* 100 (1964), p. 8-81; 101 (1965), p. 67-128.

PATZE, H., *Klostergründung und Klosterchronik*, in *Blätter für deutsche Landesgeschichte*, 113 (1977), p. 89-121.

PATZE, H., (ed.), *Geschichtsschreibung und Geschichtsbewusstsein im späten Mittelalter*, Sigmaringen, 1987.

SANCHEZ ALONSA, B., *Historia de la historiografia española. I (...1543),* Madrid, 2nd ed. 1947.

SCHARER, A., SCHEIBELREITER, G. (ed.), *Historiographie im frühen Mittelalter,* Vienna, Munich, 1994.

SCHMIDT H.J., *Die deutschen Städtechroniken als Spiegel des bürgerlichen Selbstverständnisses im Spätmittelalte*r, Göttingen, 1958 (Schriftenreihe der Historischen Kommission bei der Bayerischen Akademie der Wissenschaften, 3).

SCHNEIDER, J., *Grundlagen und Grundformen der Geschichtsschreibung im lateinischen Mittelalter,* in *Wissenschaftliche Zeitschrift der Universität Rostock*, 18 (1969), p. 483-92.

SCHNITH, K. and others, *Chronik,* in *Lexikon des Mittelalters,* 2 (1983), cc. 1954-1028.

SOT, M., *Gesta episcoporum, gesta abbatum*, Turnhout, 1981 (Typologie des sources du moyen âge occidental, 37).

SOT, M., *Un historien et son église au xe siècle: Flodoard de Reims,* Paris, 1993.

SPIEGEL, G. M., *Romancing the past. The rise of Vernacular prose historiography in thirteenth-century France,* Berkeley, 1993.

TAYLOR, J., *The Use of medieval chronicles*, London, 1965 (Helps for Students of History, 70).

TAYLOR, J., *English historical literature in the fourteenth century*, Oxford, 1987.

WATTENBACH, W., LEVISON, W., *Deutschlands Geschichtsquellen im Mittelalter. Vorzeit und Karolinger* , ed. LEVISON, W., and LÖWE, H., 5 vol., Weimar, 1952-73.

WATTENBACH, W., HOLTZMANN, R., *Deutschlands Geschichtsquellen im Mittelalter. Die Zeit der Sachsen und Salier,* ed. SCHMALE, F.-J., Darmstadt, 1967-71.

CHAPTER I

DEFINITION OF THE GENRE

A. DEFINITIONS

Although a distinction between 'histories' (*historiae*), 'annals' (*annales*) and 'chronicles' (*chronicon*) was recognised in the Middle Ages, these terms were never clearly defined. Indeed, they were used with extraordinary freedom, not only by medieval historians themselves but also by the scribes who copied their works[1].

Isidore of Sevilla went some way towards definitions in his *Etymologies* [2]. For him a chronicle was a *series temporum* of the sort written by Eusebius of Caesarea (whose work would now be called a 'world chronicle' by most scholars). Six centuries later the English historian Gervase of Canterbury (d. c. 1210) went a bit further. He felt that chronicles, as opposed to histories, should contain brief lists of events relating to kings and princes, and of portents and miracles according to the year, month and kalend in which they happened. Gervase noted, however, that authors did not always keep within the limits, as he saw them, of their chosen genre [3]. Modern historians, especially Grundmann, Guenée, Levison, van Caenegem, Genicot, Gransden and Schnith and his collaborators, have all tried hard to establish their own con-

[1] B. GUENÉE, *Histoires, annales, chroniques. Essai sur les genres historiques au Moyen Âge*, in *Annales ESC*, 28 (1973), p. 997-1016 and G. MELVILLE, *System und Diachronie. Untersuchungen zur theoretischen Grundlegung geschichtsschreiberischer Praxis im Mittelalter*, in *Historisches Jahrbuch*, 95 (1975), p. 33-67, 308-41. H. HOFMANN, *Artikulationsformen historischen Wissens in der lateinischen Historiographie des hohen und späten Mittelalter*s, in *La littérature historiographique des origines à 1500*, ed. H.U. GUMBRECHT e.a., Heidelberg,1987 (Grundriss der romanischen Literaturen des Mittelalters, vol. XI/1, t. 1.2), p. 370-83. For an example concerning the *Gesta Normannorum Ducum*, see E.M.C. van HOUTS, *Gesta Normannorum Ducum. Een studie over de handschriften, de tekst, het geschiedwerk en het genre*, Groningen, 1982, p. 144-5. I have not been able to consult *La chronique et l'histoire au Moyen Âge. Colloque du Département d'Études médiévales (mai 1982)*, ed. D. POIRION, Paris, 1984.

[2] *Isidori Hispalensis episcopi Etymologiarum sive originum Libri XX*, ed. W.M. LINDSAY, Oxford, 1911. V.28; cf. also I.41 and 44.

[3] *The Historical Works of Gervase of Canterburry*, ed. W. STUBBS. RS, London, 1879-80, 2 vol., t. 1, p. 87-8.

sensus, using modern criteria as to how the whole mass of medieval historiography is best subdivided into smaller sections, representing groups of texts having characteristics in common [4]. Even so, points of disagreement remain.

For the purpose of this work I shall define a chronicle to be a historical narrative in chronological order, covering more than one generation.

A local chronicle is written at one place, e.g. a monastery, a church, court or town, and is primarily, but not necessarily exclusively, devoted to the history of that place.

A regional chronicle is written in one region, e.g. a county, duchy or other politically coherent domain, and normally at one place within that region. It is primarily, but not necessarily exclusively, devoted to the history of that region.

The authors of local and regional chronicles normally lived in the areas they wrote about for some part of their lives at least. Most of them were men, but chronicles written by women are known too.

The above definitions are broader than some modern scholars would like. Gransden, for instance, prefers to define chronicles as serial history in which chronology dominates the narrative. She would exclude from the genre all works in which chronology is subordinate to other aspects of the narrative, e.g. to the exposition of one large theme. Thus the *Battle Chronicle* is not strictly a chronicle, according to Gransden. My broader definitions allow me to include it [5].

2. Problems of Demarcation

Having defined my brief so that it covers a wide range of works concerned with local and regional history, some of them entitled *historiae* by medieval authors and endorsed as histories by modern scholars such as Gransden, several problems arise.

First of all, many works with strong local and regional ties, which I regard as chronicles at least in part, have been discussed in earlier volumes in this series under the headings of Annals, World chronicles, Genealogies, *Gesta* of bishops and abbots or are likely to be discussed in the volume on *Historiae* which is in the course of preparation. I have to refer to these, if only to make

[4] See their works listed in the bibliography.

[5] A. Gransden, *The chronicles of medieval England and Scotland. Part I*, in *Journal of Medieval History*, 16 (1990), p. 129-30.

the reader aware of the dangers of treating one set of texts in isolation. I shall, however, focus primarily on works which have not been discussed elsewhere in the *Typologie* .

Secondly, the categories of local and regional chronicles overlap one another to a considerable extent. For example, in c. 1114 Orderic Vitalis set out to write a chronicle of his own monastery of Saint-Évroult in Normandy, but by the time he laid down his pen, shortly before he died in c. 1142, he had expanded his work chronologically and geographically into a historical narrative covering the period from the birth of Christ to his own time and concerning the whole of Western Europe[6]. As we shall see later on, it was common practice amongst chroniclers, especially those of the German towns, to put their local account into a wider regional or even national framework. Many of them also fitted their chronology into that of the Christian church by prefixing to their local chronicle an already existing world chronicle.

The third problem concerns my decision not to make too fine a distinction between certain hagiographical texts and local and regional chronicles. Many saints' lives or accounts of translations of relics are in fact histories of the institutions where the saint lived or where the relic was discovered or housed[7]. For example, the *Inventio et Miracula sancti Vulfranni* written c. 1053-4 at Saint-Wandrille in Normandy is as much a chronicle of the refoundation and growth of the monastery as it is an account of the discovery of the body of St Vulfran and of the establishment of his cult [8]. The same applies to the chronicle of the monastery of Mouzon, written about a decade earlier and concerned with the cult of St Arnulf [9]. Another reason for the frequent cross references to hagiographical works is the generic line which exists between hagiography and historiography. Several of the earliest local chronicles are institutional histories written down as serial biographies of their first abbots, modelled on saints' lives. It would be wrong to omit them from this book simply on the grounds that their model did not strictly belong to historiography.

[6] *The Ecclesiastical History of Orderic Vitalis*, ed. M. CHIBNALL , 6 vol., Oxford, 1969-80; M. CHIBNALL, *The World of Orderic Vitalis*, Oxford, 1984.

[7] See also M.HEINZELMANN, *Translationsberichte und andere Quellen des Reliquienkultes*, Turnhout, 1979 (Typologie des sources du moyen âge occidental, 33).

[8] E.M.C. van HOUTS, *Historiography and hagiography at Saint-Wandrille: the Inventio et Miracula sancti Vulfranni*, in *Anglo-Norman Studies*, XII (1989), ed. M.CHIBNALL,Woodbridge, 1990, p. 233-51.

[9] *Chronique ou Livre de fondation du monastère de Mouzon*, éd. M. BUR, Paris, 1989 (Sources d'histoire médiévale).

The last problem to be mentioned is that of the overlap between local and regional chronicles on the one hand and collections of documents pertaining to one institution on the other. The former are historical narratives in chronological order which sometimes contain the text of documents, whereas the latter consist mainly of documents with some connecting prose. The most famous examples of the latter group are the so-called cartulary chronicles of medieval monasteries and the document books of towns compiled in the later Middle Ages [10]. I shall refer to these in places in order, once again, to show how fluid the boundaries are between one historical genre and another.

C. Limitation

Having stated the difficulties of demarcation which I have encountered in planning this volume, I propose to limit myself to local and regional chronicles which lie within one of three groups: 1) chronicles of monasteries and churches in so far as they have not been discussed as part of the previously published volumes. 2) chronicles of a dynasty with particular reference to the *gesta principum*, which constitute in many cases the history of a region. 3) chronicles of towns with special reference to the ones of late medieval Germany and Italy.

[10] J. P. Genet, *Cartulaires, registres et histoire: l'exemple anglais*, in *Le métier d'historien au Moyen Âge. Études sur l'historiographie médiévale*, ed. B. Guenée, Paris, 1977, p. 95-138.

CHAPTER II

ORIGIN AND EVOLUTION

Much research and writing has been devoted to the origin of medieval historiography and to its roots in classical tradition and Christianity. A great deal of work has also been done on its evolution[1]. However, we still know rather little about how local and regional chronicles first came to be written in the early Middle Ages. There are no clear links with Roman or Byzantine traditions concerning histories of individual places of the sort which exist between medieval World chronicles and their classical precursors, and there is no evidence of a separate tradition of local and regional historiography among the Germanic peoples. The unique contribution of these peoples lies in the *origo gentis* histories which date from the sixth and seventh centuries and which are concerned only with the origins of peoples[2]. Yet, the first examples of local chronicles concerned primarily with monasteries date from these centuries too. Why did they spring up then and not earlier? We have numerous references to monasteries, family dynasties and towns in existence before the sixth centuries. Why did no one at that time write down an account of his locality and its past? These and related questions cannot be answered here but they have to be borne in mind when we survey the evidence.

A. Chronicles of a Monastery or Church

It is generally believed by scholars that the first chronicle of a monastery on the continent is the *gesta* of the abbots of Saint-Wandrille written in c.

[1] A. Ebenbauer, *Historiographie zwischen der Spätantike und den Beginn volkssprachlicher Geschichtsschreibung im Mittelalter*, in *La littérature historiographique des origines à 1500*, t. 1.1, p. 57-113.

[2] H. Grundmann, *Geschichtsschreibung im Mittelalter. Gattungen - Epochen - Eigenart* , Göttingen, 1965, p. 12-17. S. Reynolds, *Medieval origines gentium and the community of the realm*, in *History*, 68 (1983), p. 375-90. W. Goffart, *The narrators of barbarian history (AD 550-800)*. Princeton, 1988.

834-45 but this is incorrect[3]. The origin of the local monastic chronicle can be found two hundred years earlier. The chronicles of the monasteries of Condat and Agaune in the Jura, the *Vita patrum Iurensium* and the *Vita abbatum Acaunensium* date from the early sixth century. Both narratives consist of a series of lives of the first three abbots and provide an account of the spiritual needs of the pioneering monks as well as a survey of the site and of the monastery's estates. The two texts have been ignored as important evidence in the development of the historiographical genre of local history because of the impact of Bernard Krusch's opinion, now refuted, that they were not written until the 9th century[4] . Two hundred years later, but still considerably earlier than the history of Saint-Wandrille, three similar texts were written in England: Bede's prose history of the abbots of Wearmouth and Jarrow dated to 726-31, followed by two historical poems Alcuin's *Versus de patribus, regibus et sanctis Euboricensis ecclesiae*, c. 790, and the *Carmen Aethelwulfi*, written c. 803-31[5] . All three texts are local chronicles written in monasteries or churches, each devoted to the history of a single institution (though Alcuin included the succession of the Northumbrian kings).

These chronicles from the Jura and Northumbria seem to be isolated examples, unless we accept J. Hillgarth's suggestion that the writing of local *Passiones* in Visigothic Spain before 711 was a form of local historiography[6] . Early stories of martyrs certainly have some bearing on our subject; the history of monasteries and churches was often linked to the history of the saintly founder or sacred relics. It is clear from the case of the nunnery of the Holy Cross at Poitiers, however, that the lives of saints and histories of relics did not inevitably lead to chronicles of religious houses, even when the necessary documentary evidence was readily available. Gregory of Tours wrote an account of the founder, St. Radegund, in his *Historia Francorum*, and he

[3] W. WATTENBACH, W. LEVISON, *Deutschlands Geschichtsquellen im Mittelalter. Vorzeit und Karolinger*, ed. H. LÖWE, Weimar, 1957, Heft 3, p. 343-4. F.L.GANSHOF, *L'historiographie dans la monarchie franque sous les mérovingiens et les carolingiens*, in *La Storiografia altomedievale*, Spoleto, 1970, p. 657-9. M. SOT, *Gesta episcoporum, gesta abbatum*, Turnhout, 1981 (Typologie des sources du moyen âge occidental, 37), p. 34, 40.

[4] *Vie des pères du Jura* , ed. F. MARTÈNE, Paris, 1968 (Sources chrétiennes, t. 142). *Vita abbatum Acaunensium*, ed. B. KRUSCH, *MGH, SS Rer. Merov.*, t. 7, p. 322-36.

[5] *Venerabilis Baedae opera historica*,ed. C. PLUMMER, 2 vol., t. 1, p. 364-87. *Alcuin, The bishops, kings and saints of York*, ed. P. GODMAN, Oxford, 1982. *Aethelwulf de abbatibus*, ed. A. CAMPBELL, Oxford, 1967.

[6] J.N. HILLGARTH, *Historiography in Visigothic Spain*, in *La Storiografia altomedievale*, Spoleto, 1979, p. 304-5.

included several documents concerning the nunnery's foundation and early history. But none of the nuns took advantage of this material by writing a chronological account. The nearest they came to the writing of history was when Baudonivia composed a *Life of St Radegund* in c. 600[7]. Two other possible origins for monastic chronicles deserve mention. Some of them developed from annals, as Michael McCormick has described[8]. Once one set of annals was transcribed and updated in one particular monastery or church, the annals tended to lose their primary liturgical function as a means of establishing the Easter date. They became instead a framework for an account of the monastery, which could then be continued by future generations. Secondly, monastic chronicles sometimes developed from *Libri traditionum*, books recording the early grants to the institution[9]. When we turn to chronicles of secular churches or cathedrals, we notice that almost all the early ones consist of *gesta* of bishops, written in imitation of the *Liber Pontificalis*[10]. The earliest by far is the last chapter in the *Historia Francorum*, where Gregory related the history of his own cathedral to the succession of bishops. Lists of bishops exist for other cathedrals, but Gregory was the first, as far as we know, to compose a coherent chronological account[11].

From the eighth century onwards, chronicles of monasteries and churches were common. All over Europe they were written, usually after the third or fourth generation from the initial settlement, to provide the communities with a record of the foundation and donation of estates and rights. Once in existence they were regularly updated. Since monasteries and churches remained the main intellectual centres until at least the twelfth century most literary activity took place there. Besides, these institutions provided outsiders with the archival and historical material for the composition of local and regional chronicles. They acted as repositories for memorabilia of the past which they happily shared with laymen. A good example comes from 14th-

[7] *Gregorii episcopi Turonensis Libri Historiarum X*, ed. B. KRUSCH, W. LEVISON, *MGH, SS Rer. Merov.*, t. 1, p. 460-3, 468-9, 470-4. *Baudonivia, Vita sanctae Radegundis*, ed. B. KRUSCH, *MGH, SS Rer. Merov.* , t. 2, p. 377-95.

[8] M. McCORMICK, *Les Annales du haut Moyen Âge*, Turnhout, 1976 (Typologie des sources du moyen âge occidental, 14).

[9] J. KASTNER, *Historiae fundationum monasterium. Frühformen monastischer Institutionsgeschichtsschreibung im Mittelalter,* Munich, 1974.

[10] SOT, *Gesta episcoporum*, R. KAISER, *Die Gesta episcoporum als Genus de Geschichtsschreibung*, in *Historiographie im frühen Mittelalter*, ed. A. SCHARER, G. SCHEIBELREITER, Vienna, Munich, 1994, p. 459-80.

[11] Book x, c. 31, ed. KRUSCH, LEVISON, *MGH, SS Rer. Merov.*, t. 1, p. 526-37.

century Spain.

No doubt inspired by the large historiographical projects set up by King Alphonse X in Castile in the period 1252-84, King Pedro IV (Pere III) of Aragon (1336-87) commissioned the chronicle known as the *Crónica de San Juan de la Peña*. He sent researchers out to collect material from three ecclesiastical centres. The cathedral of Toledo provided all he needed to know about Visigothic Spain, the Aragonese monastery of San Juan de la Peña filled in the gaps for the past of Aragon, whereas the monastery of Ripoll handed over their Catalan version of the *Gesta comitum Barcinonensium*. So, one cathedral and two monasteries possessed between them all documents and chronicles compiled in their own houses for themselves and their friends which were put together by King Pedro's men to function as the official chronicle of the Crown of Aragon, one of our major regional chronicles from northern Spain[12] .

Another direction into which local and regional history written in ecclesiastical houses developed in the later Middle Ages can be traced in the works of Bernard Gui, the famous Dominican friar and prolific author (1261/2 - 1331). One of the projects he set up but, as far as we know, never finished was a history of the Dominican order. What he did produce was a series of short chronological accounts of each Dominican foundation in the provinces of Toulouse and Provence. Thus, the framework was very much a religious regional chronicle consisting of individual short histories [13].

B. Dynastic Chronicles and *Gesta Principum*

Chronicles centered around one family, dynasty or house often functioned as a history of the region over which that family ruled. The roots for this form of historical writing are diverse. First among them was the *origo gentis* tradition. *Origo gentis* narratives were primarily 'national' as opposed to local or regional histories, but of course all the early ones concern families which eventually produced kings. One of the earliest examples is Jordanes' *Getica*, an extract of a larger work by Cassiodore, written in c. 550[14]. Besides

[12] *Crónica de San Juan de la Peña*, ed. A. UBIETO ARTETA, Valencia, 1961 (Textos medievales, 4). P. LINEHAN, *History and the historians of Medieval Spain*, Oxford, 1993, p. 571-2.

[13] *Bernardus Guidonis de fundatione et prioribus conventuum provinciarum Tolosanae et provinciae ordinis praedicatorum*, ed. A. AMARGIER, Rome, 1961 (Monumenta ordinis fratrum praedicatorum historica, 24) and A. THOMAS, *Bernard Gui, frère prêcheur*, in *Histoire littéraire de la France*, 34 (1921), p. 139-232, esp. 193-203.

showing the origin of the Goths, Jordanes described the noble line of the Amali. Later examples are Isidore of Sevilla's History of the Visigoths and of the house of Leovigild[15], Paul the Deacon's History of the Lombards and of the house of Authari[16], and Widukind of Corvey's History of the Saxons and of the *stirps* of the Liodolfings[17]. To be classed with *origo gentis* narratives in this context are chronicles recording the rise of new dynasties. A famous example from the eighth century is the continuation, authorised by Count Childebrand, of Fredegar's Chronicle, which became a house chronicle of the Pippinids, continued under Childebrand's son Nibelung[18].

Secondly, there is evidence to suggest that vernacular songs about the deeds of individual heroes, warriors, and leaders formed another root from which dynastic chronicles sprang. In the fifthth century, Priscus referred to such songs sung to Alaric, and three hundred years later Einhard mentioned the *barbara et antiquissima carmina* about the wars and deeds of old kings which Charlemagne ordered to be written down[19]. A third root was the hagiographical tradition whereby the cult of a saint or relic became attached to one family, the history of which was then written down. The earliest known example on the Continent is the *Translatio sancti Alexandri* written at Fulda in the mid-nineth century at the request of Duke Waltbraht. It contains accounts of his grandfather Widukind, his father Wibreht and himself and thus constitutes early evidence for the wish of an aristocratic family to have

[14] *Jordanis, Getica*, ed. F. GIUNTA, A. GRILLONE, Rome, 1991 (Fonti per la Storia d'Italia, 117). For a discussion, see GOFFART, Narrators, p. 20-112. .H. ANTON, *Origo gentis - Volksgeschichte. Zur Ansein-andersetzung mit Walter Goffart's work...*, in *Historiographie im frühen Mittelalter*, ed. SCHARER, p. 262-307.

[15] *Isidori...Historia Gothorum*, ed. Th. MOMMSEN, *MGH, AA*, t. 11, part 2, p. 267-303.

[16] *Pauli Historia Longobardorum*, ed. L. BETHMANN, G. WAITZ, *MGH ,SRL*, p. 12-187; see GOFFART, *Narrators*, p. 329-431.

[17] *Widukindi Res gestae Saxonicae*, ed. A. BAUER, R.RAU, Darmstadt, 1971 (Quellen zur Geschichte der Sächsischen Kaiserzeit, ausgewählte Quellen zur deutschen Geschichte des Mittelalters, 8), p. 1-183.

[18] *The fourth Book of the Chronicle of Fredegar with its continuations*, ed. J.M. WALLACE-HADRILL, London, 1960, p. 102-3: *Vsque nunc inluster uir Childebrandus comes auunculus praedicto rege Pippino hanc historiam uel gesta Francorum diligentissime scribere procurauit. Abhinc ab inlustre uiro Nibelungo, filium ipsius Childebrando itemque comite, succedat auctoritas.*

[19] *Byzantinische Diplomaten und östliche Barbaren. Aus den Excerpta de Legationibus des Konstantinos Porphyrogennetos ausgewählte Abschnitte des Priskos und Menander Protektor*, trans. E. DOBLHOFER, Graz, 1955 (Byzantinische Geschichtsschreiber, 4), p. 54. *Einhard, Vita Karoli Magni*, c. 29, ed. L. HALPHEN, Paris, 1938, p. 82: *item barbara et antiquissima carmina, quibus veterum regum actus et bella canebantur, scripsit memoriaeque mandavit.*

their history recorded[20]. A fourth root consisted of genealogies, which have been discussed in this series by L. Genicot[21]. Genealogies developed from simple lists of names into fuller narratives when the entries for individual people were expanded into stories about their deeds. The oldest evidence, once again, concerns royal families and dates from the eighth century.

Much more research is needed to establish just how the practice of writing chronicles about ruling families derived from the roots summarised above, came to be adopted for families at a ducal, comital or lower level. The clearest surviving evidence on this matter lies in the *gesta principum* which followed the pattern set by the *gesta episcoporum* and the *gesta abbatum*. These focused on the succession of counts, dukes or kings, whose office became hereditary. The earliest example of such a chronicle at a level lower than that of kings was Dudo of Saint-Quentin's *De moribus et actis primorum Normanniae ducum* about the house of Rollo, the first viking count of Rouen[22]. His work was continued by William of Jumièges (c. 1060-1070), Orderic Vitalis (c. 1109-1113) and Robert of Torigni (c. 1139-c. 1154) until it covered the history of Normandy and, after 1066, of England also, up to the death of King Henry I (1135)[23]. Other examples date from the twelfth century and come from France or adjoining areas: they concern the lords of Guînes and Amboise, the counts of Anjou and Barcelona, and the counts and bishops of Angoulême[24]. The *gesta principum* form was also used for the English kings by William of Malmesbury (12th c.), and it was used from the

[20] B. KRUSCH, *Die Übertragung des H. Alexander von Rom nach Wildeshausen durch den Enkel Widukinds 851*, in *Nachrichten von der Gesellschaft der Wissenschaft zu Göttingen. Phil. Hist. Klasse 1933*, Berlin, 1933, p. 405-36. K. HAUCK, *The literature of house and kindred associated with medieval noble families, illustrated from eleventh- and twelfth-century satires on the nobility*, in *The medieval Nobility*, ed. T. REUTER, Amsterdam, 1979, p. 70-1.

[21] L. GENICOT, *Les généalogies*, Turnhout, 1975 and *mise à jour* 1985 (Typologie des sources du moyen âge occidental, 15).

[22] *De Moribus et Actis primorum Normanniae Ducum auctore Dudone sancti Quintini decano*, éd. J. LAIR, Caen, 1865. Also E.M.C. van HOUTS, *Gesta Normannorum Ducum. Een studie over de handschriften, de tekst, het geschiedwerk en het genre*, Groningen, 1982, p. 79-130.

[23] *The Gesta Normannorum Ducum of William of Jumièges, Orderic Vitalis and Robert of Torigni , t. 1: Introduction and Books I-IV*, ed. E.M.C. van HOUTS, Oxford, 1992.

[24] *Lambert of Ardres, Historia Comitum Ghisnensium*, ed. I. HELLER, *MGH, SS*, t. 24, p. 550-642. *Liber de compositione castri Ambaziae et ipsius dominorum gesta*, ed. L. HALPHEN, R. POUPARDIN, dans *Chroniques des comtes d'Anjou et des seigneurs d'Amboise*, Paris, 1913, p. 1-24, 74-132. *Chronica de gestis consulum Andegavorum*, ed. HALPHEN-POUPARDIN, *ibidem*, p. 25-73, 135-71. *Historia pontificum et comitum Engolismensium*, ed. J.BOUSSARD, Paris, 1957. *Gesta comitum Barcinonensium*, ed. L. BARRAU DIHIGO, J.J. MASSO TORRENTS, Barcelona, 1925.

thirteenth century onwards in Germany, Italy and Hungary[25].

However, in the later Middle Ages this genre lost much of its appeal. Many families or dynasties occupied more than one office. They extended their territories and acquired more titles. This acquisition of land and offices required either adaptation of the genre of *gesta principum* or altogether new forms of historical writing. I shall limit myself here to three examples.

About 1196, shortly after the death of Count Baldwin V of Hainault in 1195, Gilbert of Mons (d. 1224) finished his *Chronicon Hanoniense* in which he recorded the deeds of Baldwin IV and V, counts of Flanders and Hainault. He begins with an explanation about their ancestors and why they were the legitimate rulers of Hainault, a point which he repeatedly stresses. Even if he had wished to use the *gesta* genre he might have found it impossible because of the multiplicity of roles of the counts, so instead he opted for a strictly annalistic account recording their deeds mainly in Hainault. His genealogical interest, however, results in many digressions explaining the bloodrelationship between the Baldwins and other foreign families of imperial, royal and lower rank [26]. Another example concerns the *Crónica de San Juan de la Peña*, which I have mentioned earlier on. This is basically a compilation of three different local chronicles put together at the orders of King Pedro IV of Aragon to serve as a new regional history. It was easier to take over already existing chronicles and paste them together than to start from scratch by composing a coherent account of a past which was never shared. The compilation was artificial but as such it was instrumental in forging 'national' feelings centered around Pedro and his ancestors within the Crown of Aragon. For the third example we turn to the duchy of Bavaria, which was faced with another set of problems. Until 1180 it had been ruled by the Welfs. They were replaced by the Wittelsbach family with the result that who ever afterwards was writing about the dukes of Bavaria had to explain this change of dynasty. First the chroniclers of the Wittelsbach family, writing in monasteries favoured by them, manipulated the genealogies so that it looked as if the two families were related by blood and the change of dynasty the

[25] *Guilelmi Malmesburiensis Gesta Regum Anglorum*, ed. W. STUBBS, *RS*, London, 1887-9, 2 vols. *Chronicon principum Brunsvicensium fragmentum*, ed. O. HOLDER-EGGER, *MGH, SS*, t. 30, part 1, p. 21-7. *Historia ducum Veneticorum*, ed. H. SIMONSFELD, *MGH, SS*, t. 14, p. 72-89, 89-97. *P. Magister...Gesta Hungarorum*, ed. L. JUHACZ, Budapest, 1932 (Bibliotheca scriptorum medii recentisque aevorum).

[26] *La chronique de Gislebert de Mons*, ed. L. VANDERKINDERE, Brussels, 1904 (Recueil de textes pour servir à l'étude de l'histoire de Belgique).

result of regular inheritance practice. Then in the fourteenth century, especially during the reign of Louis of Bavaria (d. 1347), who became king and later emperor of the Holy Roman Empire, there was a shift of emphasis in the regional historiography from blood relationship to the place of the Wittelsbach duke as king in the long line of German kings and emperors. For example, the anonymous author of the *Chronica de gestis principum* written at Fürstefeld in 1327-8 explicitly says that he is writing about the deeds of the kings in Bavaria. In this context his choice of title is interestingly ambiguous: a *princeps* could be a duke as well as a king[27]. Finally, towards the end of the Middle Ages when the duchy was split up into four smaller units, we see a surge of national historiography of Bavaria. Instead of focusing on the family, or individual dukes or kings, the chroniclers concentrate on Bavaria as topic in itself. Obviously, as Moeglin has argued, the division of Bavaria into smaller sections made everyone wish for political unity. The historians obliged and provided unity, albeit one in the past: the *Table of Scheyern* claimed that the Wittelsbach family were descendants of the princes of Bavaria who had been given the country by Charlemagne[28].

Thus, whereas in the early and high Middle Ages local and regional chronicles concentrate on dynasties and families and the succession of office holders, in the later Middle Ages we see a gradual shift in attention to the territory itself and the events which took place regardless whether or not the ruling family was involved. This development, then, had a negative effect on the writing of dynastic history and in particular on the writing of *gesta principum.*

C. TOWN CHRONICLES

The chronicles of towns in medieval Western Europe do not appear to have sprung from classical tradition. There are of course classical histories of Rome or Constantinople, but focusing as these do on the two great centres of the Roman Empire they cannot be classed as examples of town historiography. Town chronicles may have risen from lists of consuls[29]. We have no firm

[27] *Chronica de gestis principum*, ed. G. LEIDINGER, dans *Bayerische Chroniken des XIV Jahrhunderts, MGH, SS Rer. Germ.*, 1918, p. 27-104. This section is based on J. MOEGLIN, *Les ancêtres du prince. Propagande politique et naissance d'une histoire nationale en Bavière au Moyen Âge (1180-1500)*, Genève, 1985.

[28] MOEGLIN, *Les ancêtres du prince*, p. 65-70.

[29] WATTENBACH-LEVISON, *Deutschlands Geschichtsquellen*, Heft 1, Weimar, 1952, p. 56-7.

evidence that any of these rudimentary lists, which still exist today, generated chronological accounts of towns, but such a list was undoubtedly used by Gregory of Tours. From the seventh and eighth centuries *gesta episcoporum* themselves constituted the main chronicles of many important cities in Italy, France, and Germany[30]. The succession of bishops formed a natural framework for a historical narrative about the town and diocese. In England, there is the important text of Alcuin on York from c. 790 which I have mentioned above[31]. His poem constitutes the first known example of an urban *encomium* which combines praise of a city with an account of its past[32]. Other early examples of *laudes urbium* concern Milan, written c. 738, and Verona, written c. 796-806[33]. The historical element in these poems may be small, but from poems about towns to histories of towns is but a short step. The development in Italy of town chronicles can be traced back to the eleventh and twelfth centuries, and there, as in Germany, many towns were maintaining chronicles by the fourteenth and fifteenth centuries, when the genre experienced its heyday. It is difficult to isolate the causes of the comparative lack of town chronicles from elsewhere in Europe. There is abundant evidence which illustrates the awareness of towns as political units with independent authority in Northern Europe, but somehow this awareness was not expressed in the form of chronological accounts focused on the towns as such. Admittedly, we possess important sources for the history of northern towns, such as the diaries of the Burger of Paris (15th c.) and of the Burger of Valenciennes (14th c.), both laymen; and the diary of Jean Maupoint, prior of the monastery of Sainte-Catherine-de-la-Couture (15th c.)[34], but we can-

[30] SOT , *Gesta episcoporum.*

[31] See above, p. 18.

[32] *Alcuin, The bishops*, ed. GODMAN, p. xlviii.

[33] J.K. HYDE, *Medieval descriptions of cities*, in *Bulletin of the John Rylands Library*, 48 (1965-6), p. 308-40 with inventory on p. 338-40. C.J. CLASSEN, *Die Stadt im Spiegel der Descriptiones und Laudes Urbium in der antiken und mittelalterlichen Literatur bis zum Ende des zwölften Jahrhunderts*, Hildesheim, 1980 (Beiträge zur Altertumswissenschaft, 2). P.G. SCHMIDT, *Mittelalterliches und humanistisches Städtelob*, in *Die Rezeption der Antike. Zum Problem der Kontinuität zwischen Mittelalter und Renaissance*, ed. A. BUCK, Hamburg, 1981 (Wolfenbütteler Abhandlungen zur Renaissanceforschung, 1), p. 119-28. For Verona, see Ed. E. DÜMMLER, *MGH, Poetae Latini Carolini*, t. 1, p. 118-22, and for Milan, see *ibidem*, p. 24-26.

[34] *Journal d'un bourgeois de Paris (1405-1449)* , ed. A.TUETEY (Paris, 1881), *Récits d'un bourgeois de Valenciennes* , ed. KERVYN de LETTENHOVE (Louvain, 1877) and *Journal parisien de Jean Maupoint, prieur de Sainte-Catherine-de-la-Couture (1437-1469)*, ed. G. FAGNIEZ in *Mémoires de la Société de l'histoire de Paris et de l'Île-de-France*, 4 (1877), p. 1-114.

not range them alongside with the chronicles of Genoa, Perugia, Nuremberg or Berne, which will be discussed below[35]. Antwerp provides an interesting example of another kind. Its townsclerk in the thirteenth-century was Jan van Boendale (or de Clerk). He was secretary of the *scabini* and had direct access to the town's archives. He wrote a Dutch adaptation of Jacob of Maerlant's *Spieghel Historiael*, known as the *Brabantsche Geesten (The deeds of the dukes of Brabant)*, and he also wrote several moralistic-didactic pieces in which he exalted the urban life of Antwerp. However, as Ursula Peters pointed out, he never combined his historical and urban interest for the production of a town chronicle of Antwerp[36]. Thus laymen and ecclesiastical authors gradually became interested in towns as topics in their own right, though the production of town chronicles was confined to the east and south of Western Europe. In England monastic historiography flourished in towns but only London produced texts which according to my definition can count as town chronicles[37].

[35] See below, chapter III, C.

[36] U.PETERS, *Literatur in der Stadt. Studien zu den sozialen Voraussetzungen und kulturellen Organisationsformen städtischer Literatur im 13. und 14. Jahrhundert*, Tübingen, 1983, p. 254-63.

[37] For a reconstruction of a now lost set of London Annals up to c. 1225, see M.BRETT, *The Annals of Bermondsey, Southwark and Merton*, in *Church and City 1000-1500. Essays in honour of Christopher BROOKE*, ed. D.ABULAFIA, M.FRANKLIN and M.RUBIN, Cambridge, 1992, p. 296-310.

CHAPTER III

CRITICAL OBSERVATIONS

A. CHRONICLES OF A MONASTERY OR CHURCH

1. Geography

A chronicle of a monastery or a church describes the history of the place from its foundation, or refoundation, to the author's own time. It normally covers the founding family, the first grants of land, relics and rights, and the abbots and monks and other official [1]. References to outside events or persons occur only if they are directly linked with the monastery or church. For example, the Chronicle of Bloemhof at Wittewierum written by Abbot Emo (d. 1237) is primarily concerned with his monastery and its neighbours in the Netherlands, north of Groningen, though it contains an elaborate and valuable account of the abbot's journey to Prémontré and Rome. This was the only occasion on which Abbot Emo left Groningen, but it was a business trip and therefore deserved a place in his otherwise strictly domestic narrative[2]. References to regions relatively far from the place with which the chronicle is concerned normally occur only in connection with acquisitions or loss of land in another province, pilgrimages to holy places or visits to royal or episcopal courts by members of the community, or as news brought to the community by relatives of its members or by benefactors. Thus the geographical scope of such a chronicle is determined by the extent of the community's property, its business interests and its members' contacts.

[1] H. PATZE *Klostergründung und Klosterchronik*, in *Blätter für deutsche Landesgeschichte*, 113 (1977), p. 89-121. KASTNER, *Historiae fundationum monasterium*. SOT, *Gesta episcoporum*. H.W. GOETZ, *Zum Geschichtsbewusstsein in der alemannisch-schweizerischen Klosterchronik des hohen Mittelalters (11.-13. Jahrhundert)*, in *Deutsches Archiv*, 44 (1988), p. 455-88.

[2] Ed. H.P.H. JANSEN (†), A. JANSE, Hilversum, 1990 and H.P.H. JANSEN, *Emo's emoties. De dertiende-eeuwse kroniek van Wittewierum als ego-document* , in *Bijdragen en Mededelingen betreffende de Geschiedenis der Nederlanden*, 98 (1983), p. 373-400.

2. *The past*

Where the chronicle begins with an account of the foundation, or refoundation, of the church, the circumstances leading to the first grant of land and the building of a simple structure are set out together with an account of the founder's motives. If several members of one family were concerned, a digression into the genealogy of that family tends to follow. In the cases where the founder was a saint, however, the chronicle may begin with a saint's life. Sometimes, too, we find the text of the foundation charter as a starting point. Much depends on the number of years which have elapsed between the moment of the foundation and the author's own time. The chronicles with the shortest timespan usually cover at least three generations, a point which is nicely illustrated by the earliest examples of the genre, the *Vita patrum Iurensium,* the *Vita abbatum Acaunensium* and Bede's chronicle of Wearmouth and Jarrow, which were all written during the abbacy of the fourth abbot. This fact suggests that after three generations monastic communities felt the need of written evidence to support their collective memory[3]. The authors of these early examples used the reigns of abbots as a chronological famework for their narratives, and the many *gesta* of abbots and bishops which have survived served the same purpose. Less frequently, the events narrated in chronicles were aligned with regnal dates of popes, kings or other princes.

In some cases, an author extended his house chronicle backwards in time beyond the foundation. For example, he might record the genealogy of the founder's ancestors, as Hrotsvitha of Gandersheim (d. after 973) did when she wrote the verse chronicle of Gandersheim. She did not start with the real founders Liodolf and Oda (d. 913), but with Oda's mother, Aeda daughter of Billung[4]. Or else, the author might join his account to an already existing chronicle or set of annals, to make the history of his house go back as far as the other, borrowed history. Medieval chroniclers evidently liked to start, if they could, with Christ, or earlier still with the creation of the world. For us it can be difficult to establish whether a medieval chronicler wrote his own account before adding it to an already existing one, as Orderic Vitalis did

[3] See above, p. 18, and GOETZ , *Zum Geschichtsbewusstsein*, p. 466-7 ans M. SOT, *Un historien et son église au Xe siècle: Flodoard de Reims*, Paris, 1993.

[4] *Hrotsvithae, Opera*, ed. H. HOMEYER, Munich, 1970, p. 451. P. CORBET, *Les saints ottoniens. Sainteté dynastique, sainteté royale et sainteté féminine autour de l'an Mil,* Sigmaringen, 1986 (Beihefte der *Francia*, 15), p. 111-20.

when he prefixed a World chronicle to his own, or whether he selected a suitable chronicle first and wrote his continuation afterwards, like Robert of Torigni when he added a history of King Henry I to William of Jumièges' *Gesta Normannorum Ducum* [5] .

The earliest event in the history of a monastery or church, usually its foundation, is almost invariably connected with a miracle[6]. The placing of a miracle at the beginning of a historical narrative signified that the creation of the institution was directly controlled by God. The miracle often took place in the countryside before or during a hunt. A wild animal miraculously standing still let itself be killed on the very spot where the monastery or church would be founded. Or, a brilliantly shining light would illuminate the site of the new building, as Hrotsvitha described in the case of Gandersheim[7]. The sacredness of the site provided the community with divine legitimisation for its existence.

3. The present

The authors of chronicles were often motivated by events in the present rather than the past. Not infrequently, a dispute over the acquisition or loss of property, whether in the form of land, or rights or relics, provided the stimulus. In such cases the chroniclers took pains to stress that the property, if alienated, had been lawfully acquired in the first place. An interesting example is the *Inventio et Miracula sancti Vulfranni*, the monastic chronicle and hagiographical propaganda story, written at Saint-Wandrille in c. 1053-4 to defend the monastery's allegation that it still possessed Saint Vulfran's body instead of St Peter's at Ghent which claimed it had been taken there during the viking invasions[8]. Chronicles in this class devote, not surprisingly, considerable attention to contemporary events. Since their authors were biased by their desire to justify the actions of the community their narratives were pieces of propaganda which may be slanted and unreliable.

[5] *The Ecclesiastical History of Orderic Vitalis*, ed. M. CHIBNALL, t. 1, p. 130-200. *The Gesta Normannorum Ducum of William of Jumièges, Orderic Vitalis and Robert of Torigni*, ed. E.M.C. van HOUTS, 2 vol., Oxford, 1992, 1995, t. 2, p. 196-289.

[6] KASTNER, *Historiae fundationum monasterium*, p. 94-104.

[7] P. DRONKE , *Women writers of the Middle Ages. A critical study of texts from Perpetua (d. 203) to Marguerite Porete (d. 1310)*, Cambridge, 1984, p. 75-6.

[8] Van HOUTS, *Historiography and hagiography*, p. 233-51.

Other chronicles, though not obviously biased, are sources for contemporary history for different reasons. Many were written to commemorate the death of a beloved abbot, abbess or bishop and the narrative would stop with the death of that person even if the chronicler lived on for several decades. Several chronicles betray uneasiness on the part of the authors about the political situation in which they found themselves. Erasures, rewritten passages and interlinear remarks in autograph manuscripts, which were composed over several decades, provide evidence of opinions being modified as circumstances changed[9]. Only by careful distinction of these different layers of text can we now decide which was the opinion of the original author and which was the opinion of a later scribe or interpolator. Modern historians are sometimes harsh in their judgements of their predecessors, stigmatising them as unskilled and unreliable reporters. We should remember that for them the selection of contemporary material for reportage must often have been extraordinarily difficult. Their fear of offending powerful benefactors or potential benefactors must have greatly inhibited them.

Political upheavals and natural disasters often inspired the writing of a chronicle to record a monastery's possessions. One great political upheaval was the Norman conquest of England in 1066. In the early twelfth century the monasteries of Abingdon and Ramsey and the monastic cathedrals of Ely and Rochester had cartulary chronicles compiled to record the rapid change in landholding on their estates[10]. Natural catastrophies posed another threat. Hariulf wrote a chronicle of Saint-Riquier which he interspersed with copies of documents just in case the originals would be destroyed, and the flood of 1219 at Wittewierum led Abbot Emo to record his monastery's past[11].

4. Authors and patrons

It is significant that many chronicles of monasteries and churches have survived anonymously. They were written by members of the communities out of love for God and were records of God's action on earth. Not the individual author but the community as a whole was important[12] . A touch of irony lies

[9] M.C. GARAND, *Auteurs latins et autographes des XIe et XIIe siècles*, in *Scrittura e Civiltà*, 5 (1981), p. 77-104.

[10] GENET, *Cartulaires*, p. 95-138 and GRANSDEN, *Historical writing* , t. 1, p. 270-86.

[11] *Hariulf, Chronique de l'abbaye de Saint-Riquier*, éd. F. LOT, Paris, 1894. Ed. WEILAND, *MGH, SS*, t. 23, p. 490.

[12] GRANSDEN, *The chronicles of medieval England and Scotland. Part 1*, p. 136.

behind this anonymity, for at the time the author cannot have been anonymous at all. Every single person in the monastery or church must have known his or her name. Later generations, however, forgot them.

From the names and identities which are known, it is obvious that more men than women wrote chronicles. But although they were in the minority it would be wrong to think that no female historians existed, and to argue that the chronicles surviving from medieval nunneries were all written by male chaplains rather than by the nuns themselves. I have already referred to the verse chronicle about Gandersheim written by Hrotsvitha. Other examples of local chronicles writen by women are the *Annales Mettenses priores*, the *Liber Historiae Francorum* (c. 726-7), the *Annales Quedlinburgenses* (c. 984) and the *Chronicle* of Neu-Helfta written by Abbess Sophia of Stolberg (c. 1220)[13].

The majority of chroniclers about whom we know something were people who lived or worked in the monastery or church they wrote about. Some were abbots or abbesses, like Williram of Ebersberg (d. 1085), Emo of Wittewierum (d. 1237), Sophia of Stolberg, or later became abbots, like Folcuin of Saint-Bertin (d. 990) who became abbot of Lobbes, Hariulf of Saint-Riquier (d. 1143) who became abbot of Oudenburg, and Robert of Torigni (d. 1186) monk and prior of Le Bec who became abbot of Mont Saint-Michel. Some were chanters, like Thomas of Walsingham at St Albans (d. c. 1422), or had responsibilities in the scriptorium like Orderic Vitalis (d. 1142/3) and Sigebert of Gembloux (d. 1112). Amongst the secular clergy, most chroniclers were canons, like Flodoard (966) at Reims, Bertarius at Saint-Vanne (d. after 916) and Adam (d. c. 1081) at Bremen; Hugh (d. 1139) was chanter and canon at York. But even if just monks, or nuns, they had to be well informed about the possessions of their own house. Knowledge of the charter collections must have been indispensable especially for those, like Richard of Ely, who compiled cartulary-chronicles.

Several examples are known of historians who were employed by monasteries other than their own. During a trip to his native England, Orderic Vitalis wrote about Crowland at the request of its abbot, and his contemporary William of Malmesbury (d. c. 1142) pieced together the history of Glastonbury Abbey during a two year absence from his own monastery. In both

[13] J.L. NELSON, *Perceptions du pouvoir chez les historiennes du Haut Moyen Âge*, in *Les femmes au Moyen Âge*, éd. M. ROUCHE, J. HEUCLIN, Maubeuge, 1990, p. 77-85. R. MCKITTERICK, *Frauen und Schriftlichkeit im Frühmittelalter*, in *Weiblichen Lebensgestaltung im frühen Mittelalter*, ed. H.W. GOETZ, Cologne-Vienna, 1991, p. 65-118. PATZE, *Klostergründung*, p. 115-16.

cases the chroniclers spent at least some time in the place they were writing about in order to collect material and check their sources[14].

Most chronicles were written at the request of the abbot, abbess or bishop. Even if no dedicatory letter to the head of house has survived it may often be assumed that the abbot was instrumental in initiating the work. Hrotsvitha of Gandersheim never explicitly mentioned Abbess Gerberga in her verse chronicle, as she did in the *Gesta Ottonis* which she wrote at Gerberga's request, but we may assume that the abbess encouraged both works[15]. However, some chronicles were written against the abbot or the bishop, like Richard's *Liber Eliensis*, in which the early acts of Bishop Nigel of Ely (d. 1169) are denounced[16].

There is some disagreement amongst modern historians about the extent to which chronicles of monasteries and churches are dynastic chronicles of their founding families. References to the families and their genealogies certainly form part of the chronicles, but it would be wrong to conclude with Hans Patze that they constituted the main purpose for writing the chronicles[17]. Genealogical digressions are included because the founders and benefactors formed part of the monastic *familia*, but to elevate these to the status of prime objects for the narrative would do gross injustice to the much wider objects of this form of historical writing. Also, no dedicatory letters to the lay descendants of founders have survived in these chronicles to suggest that they were written in the first instance for them.

5. *Sources*

Three different types of sources were available to the medieval local chronicler: archaeological, written and oral. The archaeological material could be found in his immediate surrounding. There were graves and tombstones inscribed with names of the deceased, inscriptions at other places and probably ruins of some sort. All these would have provided information about the history of the site. The written evidence was kept in the library and

[14] *The Ecclesiastical History of Orderic Vitalis*, ed. M. CHIBNALL, t. 2, p. 322-50. *The early History of Glastonbury. An edition, translation and study of William of Malmesbury's De Antiquitate Glastonie Ecclesiae*, ed. J. SCOTT, Woodbridge, 1981.

[15] DRONKE, *Women Writers*, p. 76-83.

[16] *Liber Eliensis*, ed. E.O. BLAKE, London, 1962, p. xlvi-xlix.

[17] PATZE, *Adels und Stifterchronik*, p. 122-7. He does not discuss this topic in his *Klostergründung*. See also KASTER, *Historiae fundationum monasterium*, p. 78-9.

archives where proprietorial marks in books together with lists of books or lists of donations would provide information about benefactors. More information concerning benefactors, however, was stored in the collections of charters recording grants and exchanges of land, rights and other transactions. And it is usually a sign of a critical mind if we find a chronicler using charter material. Most abbeys and churches kept a record of donations of relics and memorial books containing the names of those for whom the community prayed. A significant source for the past consisted of annals and chronicles written by previous generations. Some monastic chroniclers used older historiographical material which they adapted for local need and some lucky ones possessed old histories of their houses, like Hariulf of Saint-Riquier, for example, who based his work on a now lost chronicle written by Saxowalus once the monastery's chanter[18]. Others had to start from scratch, with not more than a set of annals and some saints' lives. For their own time and the very recent past the chroniclers relied heavily on oral information, which they either gathered themselves as eyewitnesses to events, like coronations, episcopal councils, dedications of churches, or on the market place, or which they received at second hand from visitors to the abbey and through relatives. Occasionally, we find chroniclers remarking on the difficulty of distinguishing between reliable and unreliable accounts. For example, Orderic Vitalis equated the former with written accounts which could be read aloud to the monks and the latter with songs sung by jongleurs[19] .

B. Dynastic Chronicles and Gesta Principum

1. Geography

Compared with chronicles of monasteries and town chronicles there are relatively few chronicles devoted to the rise of dynasties[20]. Centered round

[18] *Hariulf*, ed. LOT, p. 283.

[19] *The Ecclesiastical History of Orderic Vitalis*, ed. M.CHIBNALL, t. 3, p. 218: *Vulgo canitur a ioculatoribus de illo cantilena; sed iure preferenda est relatio autentica, quae a religiosis doctoribus sollerter est edita; et a studiosis lectoribus reuerenter lecta est in communi fratrum audientia.*

[20] HAUCK, *The literature of house*, p. 61-85. PATZE, *Adels und Stifterchronik*, 100 (1964), p. 8-81; 101 (1965), p. 67-128. MOEGLIN, *Les ancêtres du prince*. For the genre of *gesta principum*, see E.M.C. van HOUTS, *Gesta Normannorum Ducum*, p. 131-57.

one family - or the succession of one office within one family - though the dynastic chronicles are, they are also regional histories, for they describe the history of the lands ruled by the family or subjected to the office held by one of them. Their subject matter was limited by the geographical boundaries of the territory concerned. For example, the *gesta* of the counts of Guînes (c. 1200) and of the lords of Amboise (c. 1155) are devoted to events happening in a smaller area than the *gesta* of the counts of Barcelona, written c. 1162-84, or the *gesta* of the dukes of Normandy, first written c. 1060-70. Not only did the families of Guînes and Amboise hold less land, they were also less significant in political terms than the counts of Barcelona who became kings of Aragon, and the dukes of Normandy who became kings of England. The latter were prominent figures, in touch with many more people at all ranks and throughout Europe. Consequently their *gesta* and the *gesta* of other lay lords who ruled over extensive realms, cover more ground. Some such as the *Gesta Normannorum ducum* after 1066, the *Gesta comitum Barcinonensium* after 1162 or the *Chronica de gestis principum*, written shortly after Duke Louis of Bavaria, king of the Holy Roman Empire, was crowned emperor in 1328, increased dramatically in scope following the acquisition of a new title or the conquest of a new country or kingdom. The *Gesta Normannorum Ducum,* however, underwent no further expansion when Henry II became not only king of England and duke of Normandy but also count of Anjou and duke of Aquitaine. There were limits to the flexibility of the genre, if it had to be used for the deeds of one prince as lord of different territories in different capacities[21]. Similarly, the *Chronica de gestis principum* about the dukes of Bavaria focused as much on the itinerary of Louis of Bavaria as king and emperor outside Bavaria as to events which took place within the duchy[22].

Dynastic chronicles which were not written as *gesta* but in annalistic or in a loser chronological order revealed a narrative structure which was in fact opener. For example, Gilbert of Mons was so interested in showing off the well connected marriages of the princes of Hainaut that he was easily tempted to go into great detail about these foreign families. Yet, on the whole most authors did not easily go beyond the boundaries of the lands ruled by the families they described. Lambert of Waterloo reported about the members of his family for the Cambrésis, while Count Fulk le Rechin, too, con-

[21] Ed. van HOUTS, t. 1, p. xcii-xciii.

[22] MOEGLIN, *Les ancêtres du prince*, p. 51-2.

fined himself to the exploits of his ancestors in Anjou and the neighbouring provinces[23] .

Some dynastic chronicles begin with a geographical description to introduce the reader to the lands under consideration. The *gesta* of the lords of Amboise, for example, start with a detailed picture of the site of the first castle [24]. But Dudo of Saint-Quentin was more ambitious. He set out to describe the whole world before narrowing the picture to the island of Scanza, the alleged birthplace of the Norman people. Later in his chronicle he incorporated an idealized and historically inaccurate sketch of Normandy, as it was when King Charles the Simple granted it to Rollo[25]. Fictionalised or real, the territory was as much his topic as the family who ruled it. Like Dudo, Abbot John of Viktring (d. 1345) in his *Liber certarum historiarum*, also describes the world. On several occasions he quotes classical geographers presumably to convince his patrons and audience that Austria and Carinthia deserve comparison with the famous kingdoms of the past[26].

2. The past

Chroniclers who did not begin with a description of the home land usually began with an account of the earliest known ancestor. He, or she, was often a shadowy figure whose only known attribute was a name. What came next depended very much on the aspirations of the chronicler. Either he honestly confessed to ignorance of the earliest history, like the anonymous author of the *gesta* of the bishops and count of Angoulême (c. 1120-59), or he tried to fill in the gaps with tales based on local folklore or his own imagining[27]. Even in the Middle Ages, some historians were clearly sceptical about some material. Dudo of Saint-Quentin was happy to describe Rollo's adventures before he settled at Rouen, but fifty years later William of Jumièges expressed doubt about the veracity of Dudo's account and replaced it by stories about the viking invasion in general[28]. The historiography of the counts

[23] B. GUENÉE, *Temps de l'histoire et temps de la mémoire au Moyen Âge*, , in *Annuaire-Bulletin de la Société de l'histoire de France années 1976-77*, Paris, 1978, p. 30-32.

[24] Ed. HALPHEN-POUPARDIN, p. 7-8.

[25] Ed. LAIR, p. 129-31.

[26] *Iohannis Abbatis Victoriensis Liber certarum historiarum*, ed. F. SCHNEIDER, 2 vol., *MGH, SS rer. Germ.*, Hanover 1909-10, t. 1, p. 5, t. 2, p. 239-42

[27] G. DUBY, *Remarques sur la littérature généalogique en France aux XIe et XIIe siècles*, in *Académie des Inscriptions et Belles-Lettres. Comptes rendus des scéances...*, 1967, p. 123-31.

[28] *The Gesta Normannorum Ducum* , ed. van HOUTS, t. 1, p. 6.

of Anjou offers a contrasting picture as Bernard Guenée shrewdly observed. Count Fulk le Rechin (d. 1109) in his chronicle did not know his ancestor beyond Ingelger, but half a century later John of Marmoutiers reported in quite some detail on the older, but legendary, ancestor called Tertullus[29].

Most dynastic chronicles were concerned to emphazise the importance of the family and were biased in his favour. They contain many accounts of lords expanding their territory in struggles with overlords or sometimes with their own vassals, and the blame for aggression is usually laid upon the lords' neighbours. Victorious campaigns are always presented as campaigns of defence against unjust attacks. The theme of the family's role as founders and benefactors of monasteries, saviours of relics and defenders of the Church, though never insignificant, takes second place to the theme of the family's successful struggle for power.

The chronological framework was usually provided by the reigns of the lord, duke or king, but not always. Lambert of Waterloo based his chronicle on the annals of Sigebert of Gembloux, and Count Fulk le Rechin's account is a mixture of both systems. The anonymous author of the *gesta* of bishops and counts of Angoulême treated the bishops and counts in alternating chapters, roughly in chronological order.

Family chronicles usually cover three to six generations and sometimes more. It is noticable that the last two or three are normally dealt with more fully than the earlier ones. This is consistent with the pattern apparent in monastic chronicles where, as we have seen, internal evidence suggests that three generations passed before composition of a chronicle began. Authors quite often had access to information about events which occurred sixty years before their own day, in the form of eyewitness accounts of old people. Sometimes they could go back ninety years or more if old people repeated stories which they in turn had heard when they were young. One of the most famous examples of such a chain is the account of the St. Brice's Day slaughter of the Danes in England in 1002, which Henry of Huntingon (d. 1156/7) based on what old people had told him[30] .

[29] Ed. HALPHEN-POUPARDIN, p. 26-9. GUENÉE, *Histoire et culture*, p. 83. J. DUNBABIN, *Discovering a past for the French aristocracy*, in *The perception of the past in twelfth-century Europe*, ed. P. MAGDALINO, London 1992, p. 1-14.

[30] *Henrici archidiaconi Huntendunensis Historia Anglorum*, ed. T. ARNOLD, London, 1879, p. 174 : *De quo scelere in pueritia nostra quosdam vetustissimos loqui audivimus.*

2. The present

Dynastic chronicles and *gesta principum* were written with the following purposes, which were usually linked with events in the author's own time: to record and celebrate important occasions, to commemorate ancestors, to legitimise the *status quo*, as propaganda. Lambert of Waterloo explicitly mentioned the first two as his reasons for listing eighty members of his family and their deeds together with the important events of his own life[31]. The monk of Ripoll who recounted the rise of the house of Wifred the Hairy (d. 898) was celebrating the coronation of the count of Barcelona as king of Aragon in 1162, though the fact that Wifred was the founder of Ripoll Abbey provided him with an additional reason for writing[32]. The Norman conquest of England stimulated William of Jumièges to update his *Gesta Normannorum Ducum* by an account of this event. Ernst von Kirchberg wrote his vernacular verse chronicle of Mecklenburg in 1378 to celebrate Albrecht II's elevation from count to duke thirty years previously[33]. The aspects of legitimisation combined with propaganda are clearly displayed in Dudo's account of the establishment of viking rule in Normandy. He went out of his way to show that c. 911 about hundred years before his time Normandy and Brittany had been granted to Rollo as allodial possessions. In taking this stand he represented the view of his patrons, Richard I (943-96) and Richard II (996-1026) who felt great independance of the kings of France[34]. Propaganda purposes lay also behind the twelfth-century Welf material assembled as a chronicle, it seems, for Duke Henry the Black (d. 1125). The duke's deepest wish was to be the next king and emperor of the Germans and the chronicle stresses his blood relationship with members of the Liodolfing and Salian families which for centuries had produced kings[35].

[31] Ed. *MGH , SS*, t. 16, p. 549.

[32] R.J.H. COLLINS, *Charles the Bald and Wifred the Hairy*, in *Charles the Bald: Court and Kingdom*, ed. M. GIBSON, J. NELSON, BAR International Series, t. 101, Oxford, 1981, p. 169-81.

[33] *The Gesta Normannorum Ducum*, ed. van HOUTS, t. 1, p. xxxiii-xxxiv. H. PATZE, *Mäzene der Landesgeschichtsschreibung im späten Mittelalter*, in *Geschichtsschreibung und Geschichtsbewusstsein im späten Mittelalter*, ed. H. PATZE, Sigmaringen, 1987, p. 347-50.

[34] The literature on this subject is vast: for a summary and references to other literature, see D. BATES, *Normandy before 1066*, London, 1982.

[35] *Historia Welforum*, ed. E. KÖNIG, 1938 (Schwäbische Chroniken der Stauferzeit, t. 1). O.G. OEXLE, *Die "sächsische Welfenquelle" als Zeugnis der welfischen Hausüberlieferung*, in *Deutsches Archiv*, 24 (1968), p. 435-97.

Manipulation of the past in the interest of present day policies can also be found in late medieval Bavaria which was divided into four sections each ruled by different branches of the Wittelsbach family. In 1425 the last duke of the Straubing branch died and the three other dukes immediately claimed the land without succes, for it went to the Burgundians. In the same year, however, Duke Louis the Bearded of Bavaria-Ingolstadt commissioned André of Regensburg to write his *History of the dukes of Bavaria* which would show that he possessed the oldest right to the whole of Bavaria. With the help of the so-called *Table of Scheyern,* a genealogical account showing the descent of the duke directly from Bavarus, the first duke of Bavaria installed by Charlemagne, André 'proved' his master's claim[36]. The dukes in Bavaria not only faced claims from each other, they also faced claims from the emperor. Of slightly later date was the royal claim in France which precipitated the composition of the *Chronique dels comtes de Foix et senhors de Bearn.* This chronicle was written in 1443-6 as a direct result of the request from King Charles VII that the then count, Gaston IV, should commend himself to him. In fact he was asking the count to surrender the right to defend his land. Count Gaston ordered a historical enquiry into the right to style himself *comte par la grace de Dieu* and argued, successfully, that God, not the king, had given him this right and that thus the king could not claim it[37].

Sometimes the events which precipitated a dynastic chronicle did not concern the family directly. Thus it was Pope Urban II's visit to Anjou and his call for the organisation of a crusade in 1096, which led Count Fulk le Rechin to write his family's tradition[38]. After the death of William Marshall in 1219, his son commissioned a certain John to compile a family chronicle. In the event it proved to be not so much a chronicle as a biography of William, the first to be written in Old French. It covers little more than the span of William's life, though this was, admittedly, exceptionally long[39].

4. Authors and patrons

In one famous case, already referred to above, a lay aristocrat wrote his own family history, Count Fulk le Rechin (d. 1106). It was far more com-

[36] MOEGLIN, *Les ancêtres du prince,* p. 65, 75-101, 106-130.

[37] H. COURTEAULT, *Un archiviste des comtes de Foix au quinzième siècle: le chroniqueur Michel de Bernis*, in *Annales du Midi*, 6 (1894), p. 272-300.

[38] Ed. HALPHEN-POUPARDIN, p. 237-8.

[39] *L'Histoire de Guillaume le Maréchal*, éd. P. MEYER, 3 vol., Paris, 1891-1901. GRANSDEN, *Historical writing*, t. 1, p. 345-55.

mon, however, for nobles to act as patrons, by commissioning chronicles from others - sometimes from laymen and sometimes from monks or ecclesiastical officers[40]. In the eighth and ninth centuries Count Childebrand and his son Nibelung in Francia and Duke Waltbraht in Fulda acted as patrons in this way. Dudo's commission came from Duke Richard I of Normandy shortly before the duke died in 996. It was probably Richard I's great-grandson William the Conqueror who commissioned William of Jumièges to expand the *Gesta Normannorum Ducum* when he visited the abbey in July 1067, though the author does not state as much in his dedicatory letter to King William. After the death of King Henry I in 1135 his daughter Empress Matilda, together with Abbot Boso of Le Bec, persuaded Robert of Torigni to continue the *Gesta Normannorum Ducum* with a biography of Henry I. Her son in turn, King Henry II, commissioned the historians and poets Wace and Benoît to adapt the Latin *gesta* into the vernacular. Thus several members of Rollo's dynasty were actively involved in the production of chronicles of their house. Other princes who commissioned chronicles were the Welf Duke Henry the Black (d. 1125), Count Albert of Guînes (c. 1200), Albrecht II of Mecklenburg shortly before he died in 1379, the counts of Foix, Archembaud de Crailly in 1429 and Gaston IV in 1445, and several members of the Wittelsbach family in Bavaria, like Duke Louis the Bearded of Bavaria-Ingolstadt (1425), Duke Albert IV the Wise of Bavaria-Munich (1481) and his son Wolfgang in 1503[41]. After Count Fulk himself one of the authors of the Anjou *gesta* was Thomas of Loches, chaplain of Count Fulk the Young; his work was presumably commissioned by the count, though there is no firm evidence to that effect.

Dedicatory letters pose an important problem which is often difficult to solve. Did the dedicatee commission the work in question in advance, or was the work written, as it were, in the hope of future patronage? Since Dudo's work was certainly commissioned by Duke Richard I, it was presumably with future patronage in mind that he dedicated it to Bishop Adalbero of

[40] For patronage, see GUENÉE, *Histoire et culture*, p. 285-90. J. BÜMKE, *Mäzene im Mittelalter. Die Gönner und Auftraggeber der höfische Literatur in Deutschland 1150-1300* , Darmstadt, 1979. D.B.TYSON, *Patronage of French vernacular history writers in the twelfth and thirteenth centuries*, in *Romania*, 100 (1979), p. 180-222. PATZE, *Mäzene der Landesgeschichtsschreibung*, p. 331-70.

[41] OEXLE, *Die "sächsische Welfenquelle"*, p. 496-7. Ed. HELLER, *MGH , SS*, t. 24, p. 559. PATZE, *Mäzene der Landesgeschichtsschreibung*, p. 349. COURTENEAULT, *Un archiviste*, p. 280-3 and MOEGLIN, *Les ancêtres du prince*, p. 67.

Laon (977-1030). The motives of John of Marmoutiers, however, who dedicated his biography of Count Geoffrey le Bel (d. 1145) to Bishop William of Le Mans (1145-87) without explanation, need not have been the same. Abbot John of Viktring wrote dedicatory letters to Duke Albert II of Austria and an unnamed prince, as well as dedicatory poems to Bishop Bertrand of Aquilea[42].

The role of women as patrons of literature, including historiography, deserves mention. Many historical works were dedicated to women, but only a handful dynastic chronicles. Abbess Matilda of Quedlinburg (d. 999) received a copy of Widukind's history of the Saxon people, the house chronicle for the Liodolfing family, when she was thirteen, a rather young age for a patron[43]. However, her cousin Matilda abbess of Essen (d. 1011) may well have commissioned Aethelweard's Latin adaptation of the *Anglo-Saxon chronicle* which he dedicated to her. Aethelweard specifically referred to her request for information about their common ancestors - her grandmother Queen Edith (d. 946) was English - and inserted genealogies for which his chronicle is our only source[44].

A fair balance exists between secular family chroniclers and monks. Of those already mentioned André of Regensburg, Dudo of Saint-Quentin, Gilbert of Mons, Lambert of Waterloo, the anonymous author of the *gesta Pontificum et comitum Engoliensium* and Brito of Amboise were all canons, while Thomas of Loches was a comital chaplain. However, all versions of the *gesta* of the dukes of Normandy, the counts of Barcelona, at least one version of the *gesta* of the counts of Anjou, and John of Viktring's *Liber certarum historiarum* were written by monks. These examples show the significance of monasteries and churches for dynastic historiography. Not all authors came from the region about which they wrote. Dudo of Saint-Quentin worked first for the count of Vermandois and it was as that count's ambassador that he came to the ducal court in Normandy, where he spent the rest of his life, whereas Abbot John of Viktring (Carinthia), originated from Lotharingia[45].

[42] Ed. LAIR, p. 115-20. Ed. HALPHEN-POUPARDIN, p. 172-5. Ed. SCHNEIDER t. 1, p. 141-6, t. 2, p. 238-46.

[43] *Widukindi res gestae Saxonicae*, ed. BAUER-RAU; the prefaces addressed to Abbess Matilda can be found on p. 16, 82 and 124.

[44] *The Chronicle of Aethelweard*, ed. A. CAMPBELL, London, 1962, p. 1-2. E.M.C. van HOUTS, *Women and the writing of history in the early Middle Ages: the case of Abbess Matilda of Essen and Aethelweard*, in *Early Medieval Europe*, 1 (1992), p. 53-68.

[45] Ed. LAIR, p. 294-5. and Ed. SCHNEIDER, t. 1, p. v.

5. Sources

The information given above concerning the sources for monastic chronicles applies also to dynastic chronicles, and it needs no repetition. It is worth noting, however, that family chroniclers are relatively forthcoming about their oral informants, as the following will show[46].

Dudo of Saint-Quentin explicitly mentioned Count Radulf of Ivry (d. after 1011) and Countess Gunnor (d. 1031), respectively half-brother and wife of Duke Richard I, as the informants on whose stories and memory he relied[47]. In his prologue, John of Marmoutiers listed by name and status six persons from the entourage of Count Geoffrey le Bel (d. 1145) as being informants who had contributed details about his life[48]. Count Fulk le Rechin briefly mentioned in the course of his chronicle that he wrote the history of his family according to oral information given to him by his uncle Count Geoffrey Martel who had died thirty-six years previously in 1060[49]. Lambert of Waterloo too relied on details of his family provided by his uncle Radulf[50]. A large section of Lambert of Ardres' *gesta* of the counts of Guînes is based on oral stories provided by Walter of Clusa, an illegitimate son of Count Albert of Ardes[51]. So it seems that every aristocratic family had at least one member who was particularly interested in preserving family history.

Family traditions may of course have been written down informally before they were included in chronicles. Simple lists of names and rudimentary genealogies probably existed from the ninth century onwards. Robert of Torigni included eight such lists and genealogies in his version of the *Gesta Normannorum Ducum* and the information which they contain is on the whole reliable[52]. We know that on her deathbed Queen Matilda (d. 969),

[46] For oral traditions as a historical source, see GUENÉE, *Temps de l'histoire*, p. 34-5, *Histoire et culture*, p. 78-85 and B. STOCK, *The implications of Literacy. Written Language and Models of Interpretation in the eleventh and twelfth centuries*, Princeton, 1983, p. 42-87. See also M. RICHTER, *The oral Tradition in the early Middle Ages*, Turnhout, 1994 (Typologie des sources du moyen âge occidental, 71).

[47] Ed. LAIR, p. 125: *versus ad comitem Rodulfus hujus operis relatorem;* p. 289: *capacisque memoriae et recordationis thesauro profusius locupletae.*

[48] Ed. HALPHEN-POUPARDIN, p. 174.

[49] *Ibidem*, p. 232: *sicut ille meus avunculus Gosfridus Martellus narravit mihi.*

[50] Ed. WEILAND, *MGH , SS*, t. 16, p. 511-12.

[51] Ed. HELLER, *MGH , SS*, t. 24, p. 607.

[52] E.M.C. van HOUTS, *Robert of Torigni as genealogist*, in *Studies in Medieval History presented to R. Allen BROWN*, ed. C. HARPER-BILL, C. HOLDSWORTH and J. NELSON, Woodbridge, 1989, p. 216-33.

widow of King Henry the Fowler, handed a roll to her granddaughter Matilda, abbess of Quedlinburg, on which were inscribed the names of dead noblemen, and that she asked Matilda to pray for their souls and for the souls of her husband and herself[53]. Queen Matilda's great-granddaughter, Abbess Matilda of Essen, was instrumental as we have seen in the recording of ancestors, and also of the names of her English cousins related to her through her British grandmother Queen Edith. Women, unlike men, did not fight and were not killed in military engagements. It was particularly their task, therefore, to keep family traditions alive and to pass them on to others for remembrance in writing and in prayer. It was also their task to instruct their sons concerning the exemplary deeds of their ancestors.

C. Town Chronicles

1. Geography

Town chronicles are focused on the history of one town and its principal inhabitants. As in the case of chronicles of monasteries or churches we hear about 'external' affairs only in sofar these were directly linked to events in the town[54]. Chronicles written in large harbour towns, like the Italian cities of Genoa,

[53] *Vita Mahthildis reginae antiquior*, ed. R. KOEPKE, *MGH , SS*, t. 10, p. 581: *Quin etiam computarium, in quo erant nomina procerum scripta defunctorum, in manum ipsius dans, animam illi commendavit Heinrici nec non et suam, sed et omnium quorum ipsa memoriam recolebat fidelium.*

[54] For Germany' see H. J. SCHMIDT, *Die deutschen Städtechroniken als Spiegel des bürgerlichen Selbstverständnis im Spätmittelalter*, Göttingen, 1958. F. Du BOULAY, *The German town chroniclers*, in *The writing of history in the Middle Ages. Essays presented to Richard William SOUTHERN*, ed. R.H.C. DAVIS, J.M. WALLACE-HADRILL, Oxford, 1981, p. 445-69. K. WRIEDT, *Geschichtsschreibung in den wendischen Hansestädten*, in *Geschichtsschreibung und Geschichtsbewusstsein im späten Mittelalter*, ed. H.PATZE, Sigmaringen, 1987, p. 401-426. For Switzerland, see J.P.BODMER, *Chroniken und Chronisten im Spätmittelalter*, Bern, 1976 (Monographien zur Schweizer Geschichte herausgegeben von der allgemeinen Geschichtforschenden Gesellschaft der Schweiz, 10). For Italy, see E. COCHRANE, *Historians and historiography in the Italian Renaissance*, Chicago, 1981, esp. 1-162. L.GREEN, *Chronicle into history. An essay on the interpretation of history in Florentine fourteenth-century chronicles*, Cambridge, 1972. G. MARTINI, *Lo spirito cittadino e le origini della storiografia communale lombarda*, in *Nuova Rivista Storicà*, 54 (1970), p. 1-22. U.LINK-HEER, *Italienische Historiographie zwischen Spätmittelalter und früher Neuzeit*, in *La littérature historiographique des origines à 1500*, ed. H.U. GUMBRECHT, U.LINK-HEER, P.M. SANGENBERG, Heidelberg, 1988 (Grundriss der romanischen Literaturen des Mittelalters, vol. XI/1), t. 1.3, p. 1067-1130.

Pisa and Venice, nevertheless contain much information about the rest of Italy, the Mediterranean, and Europe because these cities had trading contacts.

The earliest known chronicle from Italy to be started as a town chronicle rather than as a *gesta episcoporum*, was begun in the first half of the twelfth century in Genoa by Gaffaro (d. 1166)[55]. On his own initiative he set out to write a record of the Genoese contribution to the first Crusade, and when the work was finished, in 1152, he offered it to the commune of Genoa. The leaders of the commune decided to have it copied and deposited in the city archives and it grew into the town's official historical record continued up to 1293. Its opening sections, from 1099 onwards, deal as much with the Holy Land as with Italy, but Genoa is nevertheless the theme.

The chronicles of towns which had no direct access to the sea and did not trade on a large scale tell us about rivalry with neighbouring towns and disputes with landed aristocracy nearby, and about the negotiations and warfare involved. Thus in Erhard Schürstab's account of Nuremberg we find details of war with Count Albrecht of Brandenburg in 1449-50[56], and in the anonymous chronicle of Brunswick the continuous tension between the town authorities and the Welf dukes is a major theme[57]. References to kings and emperors and thus to the larger concept of kingdom and empire occur sporadically, usually when royal election, coronations or death take place in or near the town in question[58]. One important exception to this rule is the *Cronica Maiorum et Vicecomitum Londoniarum* , written between 1258 and 1272, probably by the alderman of Bridgeward, Arnold Fitz Thedmar. Although primarily interested in London itself and the abbeys nearby, it contains important and unique evidence for the history of Germany because of the election of Richard of Cornwall as king there. Arnold used Richard's correspondance with the city and three of his letters have survived only as part of the *Cronica*[59].

[55] *Annali Genovesi di Gaffaro e de' suoi continuatori dal MXCIX al MCCXCIII*, ed. L.T. BELGRANO, C. Imperiale di Sant' Angelo (Fonti per la Storia d'Italia), 5 vol., 1890-29, t. 1, p. 1-75 (original text).

[56] *Die Chroniken der deutschen Städte von 14. bis in 16. Jahrhundert [CDS]*, ed. Historische Kommission bei der Bayerischen Akademie der Wissenschaften. Leipzig, 1862 - .... Last volume is t. 37 on Bremen published at Bremen in 1968. For Schürstab's chronicle, see *CDS*, t. 2, p. 123-352 .

[57] *CDS*, t. 6, p. 25-120 at p. 25-7.

[58] Du BOULAY, *The German town chroniclers*, p. 452. For royal entrées in France, see B. GUENÉE, F. LEHOUX, *Les entrées royales françaises de 1318 à 1515*, Paris, 1968.

When the Dominican chronicler Johann Nederhoff embarked upon his chronicle of Dortmund he did so, he tells us, because he had failed to find any information about the town's history in the works of Vincent of Beauvais, Martin of Troppau and Henry of Herford[60]. His failure is no surprise: all those works were world chronicles, written on too large a scale to provide the sort of detail for which Johann Nederhoff was searching. It is worth noting, however, that his first thought was to look at previous chronicles rather than to examine the libraries and archives of Dortmund itself.

b. The past

The time spans of town chronicles vary greatly according to their nature. Some of them are almost to be classified as family chronicles, because they are constructed around the genealogy of an important family within the town and for these a span of about 150 years is typical. One example is the chronicle of Nuremberg which Ulman Strömer wrote between 1360 and his death in 1407; this is largely concerned with the history of his own family, one of the most important of Nuremberg, which he traced back to the beginning of the thirteenth century[61] . Another is Hector Mülich's chronicle of Augsburg from 1348 to 1487. John Kerkhörde's work on Dortmund covers only sixty years, however, from 1405 to 1465[62]. At the opposite extreme, some families tried to boost their importance by tracing their ancestry back to the Romans as did the fifteen families in Cologne who claimed descent from the Emperor Trajan[63]. Patrician families, whose members were often officials on the towns' councils, happily invoked legend and myth to legitimize their actions. An early example can be found in late eleventh-century Trier, where the idea emerged that the town's founder was Trebetus, son of the Babylonian king Ninus and stepson of Queen Semiramis. This legend enabled Trier's citizens to boast that it was 1250 years older than Rome. Trier's campaign to proclaim itself as a rival Rome north of the Alps rested largely on this supposed

[59] *De Antiquis Legibus Liber: Cronica Maiorum et Vicecomitum Londoniarum...cum appendice,* ed. T. STAPELTON, London, 1846, p. 1-177. For the letters and affairs in the Holy Roman Empire, see p. 26-9, 133-5. GRANSDEN, *The writing of history*, t., 1, p. 509-17.

[60] SCHMIDT, *Die deutschen Städtechroniken*, p. 15 and note 9.

[61] *CDS*, t. 1, p. 25-106 and Du BOULAY, *The German town chroniclers,* p. 449.

[62] *CDS*, t. 22, p. 1-273 (Augsburg); *CDS*, t. 20 , p. 25-146 (Dortmund).

[63] F. GRAUS, *Funktionen der spätmittelalterlichen Geschichtsschreibung,* in *Geschichtsschreibung und Geschichtsbewusstsein*, ed. H. PATZE, p. 50 and note 230.

seniority[64]. There are plenty of other examples of towns which sought their origin in a past which was older than that of Rome. In Italy itself there was fierce competition. Perugia claimed that it had been founded by Eulistes, who had fought and conquered the Trojans. His exploits were described by Bonifacius of Verona in a Latin epos *Eulistea*, or *De rebus a Perusinis gestis*, written shortly after 1293.

Town chronicles which were less clearly concerned with individual families were not infrequently produced, as were monastic and dynastic chronicles, by ingenious adaptation to local circumstances of pre-existing models. Examples of town chronicles produced by adaptation of (world) chronicles are the chronicle of Strassbourg by Jacob Twinger of Königshofen[65] and the chronicle of Lübeck which the Franciscan Detmar extended in about 1400, using an earlier version which covered the period from 1101 to 1347; Detmar's source, which is now lost, was clearly modelled on Helmold's *History of the Slavs*[66]. The citizens of London, the only city in England which had its own urban chronicle tradition, used Matthew Paris' *Flores Historiarum* as the basis of their local chronicle, and by doing so they acquired a ready made past from the Creation to 1258, which they then brought up to date[67]. In Genoa, Caffaro went back only to 1099, but his chronicle was used as a base for many subsequent works[68] . When Bonvesin da la Riva (d. 1313) wrote his eulogy of Milan in 1288, he traced its history on a global scale back to the Roman empire but gave detailed notes only for the last two hundred years[69]. One of the longest and most extensive town chronicles was Giovanni Villani's history of Florence, in twelve books full of legendary and romantic stories connecting Florence with Fiesole and Fiesole with Antenor and Troy[70].

[64] Ed. G. WAITZ, *MGH, SS*, t. 8, p. 130. H. THOMAS, *Studien zur Trierer Geschichtsschreibung des 11. Jhs insbesondere zu den Gesta Trevorum*, Bonn, 1968.

[65] *CDS*, t. 8, p. 230 to t. 9, p. 916. F. HOFINGER, *Studien zu den deutschen Chroniken des Fritsche Closener von Strassburg und des Jacob Twinger von Köningshofen*, Munich, 1974.

[66] WRIEDT, *Geschichtsschreibung*, p. 401-26. For the use of world chronicles for regional history, see P. JOHANEK, *Weltchronistik und regionale Geschichtsschreibung im Spätmittelalter*, in *Geschichtsschreibung und Geschichtsbewusstsein*, ed. PATZE, p. 287-330.

[67] GRANSDEN, *The chronicles of medieval England and Scotland. Part 1*, p. 132 and BRETT, *The Annals of Bermondsey*, p. 296-310.

[68] Ed. BELGRANO, t.1, p. 3.

[69] *Bonvesin da la Riva, De magnalibus Mediolani. Le meraviglia di Milano*, ed. G. PONTIGGIA, M. CORTI, Milan, 1974.

[70] Ed. F. GHERARDI DRAGOMANNI 4 vol., Florence, 1844-5 (Reprint Frankfurt, 1969) and LINK-HEER, *Italienische Historiographie*, p. 1078-87.

The Venetian *Doge* Andrea Dandolo (d. 1354) wrote his *Chronicon Venetum* entirely as a history of the past up to 1280, and he then wrote a separate chronicle covering the years 451 to 1342 in which he dealt with his own time[71].

3. The present

Many chroniclers wrote to glorify the towns to which they themselves belonged and were clearly motivated by pride, a pride often stimulated by contemporary events. Thus it was the First Crusade and Genoa's financial and military contribution to the fleet and army, which inspired Caffaro, who was one of the organisers, to start the record of events which became the chronicle of Genoa[72] . From later centuries we have the examples of Bonvesin da la Riva in Milan and Giovanni Villani (d. 1348) in Florence whose pride in their own cities shines from their pages. Bonvesin, a member of the Third Order of the Umiliati, wrote his *De magnalibus Mediolani* in 1288. In eight books he described both the city and its economic wealth in his own time. The chronicle proper, covering the period from 1168 onwards, is embedded in chapter five and comprises one third of the whole work. Of his work, therefore, the bulk is contemporary history[73]. Bonvesin's younger contemporary from Florence, Giovanni Villani (1276-1348) also wrote for patriotic reasons. He was a layman and a partner in one of the Florentine merchant banks, and the chronicle which he composed in 1338 is interspersed with statistics of the city's wealth. He was especially stirred by the enormous sums which Florence spent on its wars with Verona. A businessman himself, he was influenced by the genre of the *ricordanze*, or business diaries, kept by many families as records of their affairs. Sometimes such diaries turned directly into local chronicles, which were updated from generation to generation[74]. No such evidence survives from England, though the *Cronica Maiorum et Vicecomitum Londoniarum*, by times reads as a diary of

[71] *Andreae Danduli Chronicon per extensum descripta*, ed. E. PASTORELLO, in *Rerum Italianorum Scriptores*, n.s., t. 12, 1, p. 1-327. *Andreae Danduli Chronica Brevis*, ed. E. PASTORELLO, *ibidem*, p. 351-73.

[72] J.K. HYDE, *Society and Politics in Medieval Italy. The Evolution of civil Life, 1000-1350*, ,London, 1973, p. 51-2. COCHRANE, *Historians*, p. 60-2.

[73] Ed. PONTIGGIA-CORTI, p. 110-59.

[74] P.J. JONES, *Florentine families and Florentine diarists in the 14th century*, in *Papers of the British School at Rome*, 24 (1956), p. 183-205.

the author Arnold Fitz Thedmar who seems to have been particularly interested in the enforcement of laws regulating the assize of weights and measures to stop bakers selling short weight.

Wars between cities formed an important stimulus for the writing of town chronicles. In Switzerland the compilation of a chronicle of Berne followed from the town council's initiative after the victory of the Aargaus in 1418. The town's officials approached a former town's scribe Konrad Justinger who had learned his craft in the office of Jakob Twinger in Strassbourg. At his own initiative he had already compiled a chronicle of Berne three years previously, which was in fact more or less a continuation of Twinger's own work. Justinger's chronicles in turn were used as the basis for another set of two chronicles written as celebrations after the Burgundian war of 1477. The author was Diebold Schillung who apart from his other qualities was also a skilled painter who magnificently illustrated one of his chronicles *mit me dan sechshundert kostlicher figuren*[75]. In Germany the Savoye war formed the immediate cause for Fribourg's historiography in 1447-8, while the internal strife in Mainz between the patricians and the guilds led to a series of chronicles starting respectively in 1332, 1428-9 and 1444-5[76]. In those cases where war provided the incentive, accounts of the contemporary period take up the largest part of the chronicle, naturally so, since the towns' officials were responsible for keeping records of recruitment, casualties and other military details[77] .

4. Authors and patrons

A substantial number of chronicles were written by important patricians who themselves took active part in the town's government, for example Caffaro (Genoa), Strömer (Nuremberg), Villani (Florence), Fitz Thedmar (London), Dandolo (Venice) and Hinrik Lange (d. 1455/6) (Lüneburg). In all these cases the authors themselves took the initiative[78]. To what extent they were supported by scribes, researchers or other helpers we do not know, although in the case of Caffaro it is conceivable that after 1152 the *scribanus publicus*, the town's notary who was commisioned to copy Caffaro's work,

[75] *Konrad Justinger, Die Berner Chronik nebst 4 Beilagen...*, ed. G. STUDER, Bern, 1871. BODMER, *Chroniken und Chronisten im Spätmittelalter* , p. 11-16, 41-42.

[76] GRAUS, *Funktionen*, p. 48 and note 214. *CDS*, t. 18, p. 315-20 (Mainz).

[77] *CDS*, t. 20, p. 452-5 (Neuss) and t. 21, p. 5-171 (Soest).

[78] For Lüneburg, see *CDS*, t. 36, p. 163-274.

continued the chronicle into its second part, which ends in 1163, either on his own or under Caffaro's supervision[79].

Many chronicles from Italian, Swiss or German towns were written by the towns' scribes and notaries. These were officials paid by towns to undertake administration and keep records. The role of notaries in this respect needs more investigation. Arnaldi has suggested that they were commissioned to write chronicles because one of their tasks was to authenticate documents, and because any account of the past which a notary produced would therefore be accepted as being beyond dispute[80] .

Town chronicles were also written on commission by members of the clergy and in particular the mendicant orders took the initiative for urban historiography. I have already referred to the Franciscan Detmar. He was commissioned in 1385 to write his chronicle of Lübeck by the town's council. The lost chronicle which he extended was probably composed in the 1340s by a member of the same order in the Franciscan monastery of St. Catherine's[81] . The first town chronicle of Strassbourg was composed by yet another Franciscan, Closener, as we have seen. Küchlin, author of the Augsburg chronicle, was a priest. He wrote at the instigation of the patrician Burgomaster Peter Egen (d. 1452). According to Küchlin, Peter Egen commissioned the work because he liked to decorate his house with scenes from the past [82].

Finally, some town chroniclers were poets as much as historians: they wrote in the vernacular and they wrote in rhyme. One of these was Gotfrid Hagen who composed a *boich von der stede Colne* between 1277 and 1287. It deals mainly with the struggle between the town and the archbishops Conrad of Hochstaden and Engelbert of Falkenberg during the years 1252 and 1271[83]. A rhyme chronicle and a prose chronicle were written in parallel in

[79] G.ARNALDI, *Studi sui cronisti della Marca Trevigiana nell' età di Ezzelino da Romano*, Rome, 1963, p. 225-45.

[80] G.ARNALDI, *Il notaio-cronista e le cronache cittadine in Italia*, in *La storia del diritto nel quadro delle scienze storiche. Atti del primo congresso internazionale della Società Italiana di Storia del Diritto*, Florence, 1966, p. 293-309.

[81] WRIEDT, *Geschichtsschreibung*, p. 401-26. See also, SCHMIDT, *Die deutsche Städtechroniken*, p. 27-8.

[82] *CDS*, t. 4, p. 333.

[83] *CDS*, t. 12, p. 22-200 (Hagen's chronicle). For the genre of rhyme chronicles, see also S.B. JANSONN, *Medeltidens rimkröniker. Studier i funktion, stoff, form,* Stockholm, 1971 (Studia litterarum Upsaliensia, t. 8) and A.H.L. HAGE, *Sonder favele, sonder lieghen. Onderzoek naar vorm en functie van de middelnederlandse rijmkroniek als historiografisch genre*. Groningen, 1989.

the town of Soest [84]. There is also evidence that town chroniclers wrote poems celebrating political victories, or indeed, worked as literary authors in general for a predominantly lay urban audience[85].

5. Sources

Although many town chronicles are based upon pre-existing world chronicles or similar works of wide geographical scope, their authors clearly had access to other sources, on which they relied for information of a local nature. Some of these were narrative sources, such as annals, diaries, hagiographical accounts, usually linked with the patron saints of the town and its churches, and genealogies for the town-family chronicles. Other documentary sources included the so-called town books in Germany *(Stadtbücher)*, preserved in many German archives, which contained records of administration, rules for law and order, accounts of feuds, military information concerning recruitment and the like, lists of officials, tax records, and of course charters. Private business accounts or diaries, like the *ricordanze* I have already mentioned, were sometimes available. Last, but not least, town chroniclers relied on oral stories. Since most of them were either important patricians or town officials, they were well placed to gather information and to report on events they had witnessed themselves.

[84] *CDS*, t. 21, p. 5-167, 282-336.

[85] HOFMANN, *Artikulationsformen*, p. 639-42 and PETERS, *Literatur in der Stadt*, p. 234-40.

CHAPTER IV

PUBLIC AND RECEPTION

A. LANGUAGE

Until the middle of the twelfth century all chronicles were written in Latin, except in England where the *Anglo-Saxon Chronicle* existed in the vernacular. That Latin presented no problem for monastic audiences seems obvious, but was the same true for lay people? This is a difficult question to answer, particularly in the context of dynastic chronicles. We have seen that many of these were commissioned by lay aristocrats who wished to be informed about their past and to keep family traditions alive for future generations. Even if we agree with Rosamond McKitterick's concept of 'pragmatic literacy' that many lay magnates knew enough Latin to be able to follow legal documents and to issue simple orders in that language, it is very difficult to believe that they could have understood literary Latin in its more complex forms[1]. The language of the *Continuation of Fredegar's Chronicle* commissioned by Count Childebrand is more difficult than the language used in Charlemagne's *Capitularia* but still considerably easier than the 'hermeneutic' style of Dudo of Saint-Quentin's *gesta* of the dukes of Normandy[2]. The Latin dynastic chronicles, then, were probably translated or more freely adapted into the vernacular orally for their lay audiences. We have to remember here that some chroniclers specifically stated that they had received their information orally, much of it from members of the lay aristocracy. These nobles presumably communicated their historical information in the vernacular, and it is reasonable to suppose that they required the information of

[1] R. MCKITTERICK, *The Carolingians and the written word*, Cambridge, 1989, p. 227-70 and *The audience for latin historiography in the early middle ages: text transmission and manuscript dissemination*, in *Historiographie im frühen Mittelalter*, ed. SCHARER, SCHEIBELREITER, p. 96-111. B. STOCK, *The implications of literacy. Written language and models of interpretation in the eleventh and twelfth centuries*, Princeton, 1983, p. 12-87.

[2] For Dudo's language, see M. LAPIDGE, *The hermeneutic style in tenth-century Anglo-Latin literature*, in *Anglo-Saxon England*, 4 (1975), p. 67-111.

others to be fed to them in the vernacular too. The written narrative was, however, in Latin.

However, this was not the case for long, for by the end of the twelfth century vernacular histories were appearing in the form of rhyme chronicles. They emerged as adaptations of Latin dynastic chronicles simultaneously in the Anglo-Norman realm and in Germany. The *Roman de Rou* of Wace, written c. 1160-74, and the *Chronique des ducs de Normandie*, written c. 1187, were commissioned by King Henry II of England (1154-87), whereas the *Kaiserchronik*, written c. 1160-89, originated at Regensburg[3]. Despite the rise of the vernacular the demand for Latin did not immediately diminish, as is shown by a Spanish example. Between 1248 and 1305 Jofré da Loaisa, archdeacon of Toledo, wrote a chronicle of the kings of Castilla in Catalan. This proved to be so unpopular that the author himself commissioned Armand of Cremona to produce a Latin translation[4]. As far as the substantial volume of fifteenth-century Bavarian dynastic historiography is concerned, J. Moeglin has pointed out that initially the lay historians wrote their work directly in the vernacular, whereas the two main ecclesiastical writers, André of Regensburg and Veit Arnpech stuck to Latin. Within a few years, however, the latter two were more or less forced by their lay audiences to produce German translations[5]. The earliest town chronicles were all written in Latin and the first translations date from the 14th century. The earliest known example there is Closener's chronicle of Strassbourg which was followed immediately by that of Jakob Twinger, who explained in his preface that he wrote especially for the learned laity[6]. He was one of a group of chroniclers

[3] *Le Roman de Rou de Wace*, ed. A.J. HOLDEN, 3 vol., Paris, 1970-3. *Chronique des ducs de Normandie*, ed. C. FAHLIN, 2 vols, Uppsala, 1951-2. *Die Kaiserchronik von Regensburg*, ed. E. SCHRÖDER, *MGH, Dt Chron.*, t. 1. LINEHAN, *History and the historians of Spain*, p. 446-8.

[4] *Crónica, J. de Loaisa: estudio preliminar, edicion e indices*, ed. A. UBIETO ARTETA, Valencia, 1971 (Textos medievales, 30). *Jofré de Loaysa, Cronica de los reyes de Castilla*, ed. A. GARCIA MARTINEZ, Murcie, 1982, 2nd ed. For prose chronicles, see G.M. SPIEGEL, *Romancing the past. The rise of vernacular prose historiography in thirteenth-century France*, Berkeley, 1993.

[5] J. MOEGLIN, *Les ancêtres du prince*, p. 65-6, 69-70.

[6] *CDS*, t. 8, p. 230-1: " Man findet geschriben in latyne vil kroniken, das sind bücher von der zit, die do sagent von keysern, bebesten, künigen und von andern fürsten und herren, wie ir leben si gewesen, und von etlichen neuhaftigen dingen die von in oder bi iren ziten geschehen sint. Aber zü dütsche ist lüzel sollicher bücher geschriben, wie doch das die klügen legen also gerne lesent von semelichen dingen also gelerte pfaffen."

who wrote both in Latin and in the vernacular and whose vernacular work was much more widely read[7].

B. CONTINUATIONS

Most chronicles were continued in one way or another. The annalistic style of entries year by year as well as the *gesta* form of serial biographies encouraged expansion. Local chronicles were usually continued in the monastery, church or town where they had first been written; a member of the next generation updated the existing version by adding new information at the end. There is some evidence to suggest that in monasteries the task was assigned to monks with historical interest early on in their career and that, in other words, updating and continuing was part of the job of the 'apprentice' chronicler. Both Orderic Vitalis and Robert of Torigni, important twelfth-century historians, updated and interpolated the annals in their monasteries of Saint-Évroult and Le Bec as well as William of Jumièges' *Gesta Normannorum Ducum* before they wrote their own major works[8] .

Normally, updating a chronicle posed no problems. In some circumstances, however, e.g. during times of war, political tension or after a change of dynasty when partiality was difficult to maintain, the chronicler found it prudent to concentrate upon interpolation: it was safer to describe the past than to commit himself by writing contemporary history. Interpolations consisted of information which the original, contemporary public had not needed, but which through the passage of time had become necessary for a new generation. In addition, they often contained arguments or opinions to balance the original verdict of the chronicler. A good example, here, is the work of Orderic Vitalis in interpolating the *Gesta Normannorum Ducum*. Within forty years after William of Jumièges, he judged it necessary not only to fill in gaps in the original brief account of the Norman conquest of England, but also more significantly for us to tone down William's pro-Norman point of view[9].

Regional chronicles, and particularly dynastic chronicles, were often continued and interpolated in other places besides, or instead of, their place of origin. Because they dealt with a larger geographical area than the avarage

[7] D.J. PONERT, *Deutsch und Latein in deutscher Literatur und Geschichtsschreibung des Mittelalters*, Stuttgart, 1975 (Studien zur Poetik und Geschichte der Literatur, t. 43).

[8] *The Gesta Normannorum Ducum*, ed. van HOUTS, t. 1, p. lxvii, lxxviii-lxxix.

[9] *Idem*, p. lxxiii-lxxiv.

institutional chronicle, more monasteries needed to possess copies, which they then updated separately. The process of continuation of the *Gesta comitum Barcinonensium* appears to have been limited to the monastery of Ripoll, where it originated, though there is some evidence which points to Cuixa.The text became widely known, however, when, in a condensed form, it was incorporated in the *Crónica de San Juan de la Peña*[10]. The *Gesta Normannorum Ducum* was not continued at Jumièges. The later versions of it stem principally from other monasteries in Normandy, like Saint-Ouen at Rouen, Saint Évroult and Le Bec; but one redaction originated outside Normandy, and there were plans for an Anjevin continuation[11]. The textual tradition of the *gesta* of the counts of Anjou presents a similar picture of continuations composed at Loches, Marmoutiers and Amboise[12]. Rhyme chronicles, however, were not continued on the same scale as the Latin chronicles, presumably because their structure was thought to be less open-ended.

Once a chronicle had left its place of origin, the original author lost sight of it and had no control over it. Every scribe was in effect free to add, interpolate and alter the text as it pleased him. Copyright in the modern sense did not exist. The original text and its continuations were treated as one collective product. This is borne out by the fact that anonymous redactors often preserved the original author's references to himself in the first person singular. They referred to themselves in the same way and made no attempt to explain which opinions belonged to one author and which to another, making it very difficult for us to distinguish between them. Only for chronicles such as Caffaro's account of Genoa where each of Caffaro's successors wrote down his name and title at the beginning of his contribution, is it a straightforward matter to disentangle layers of authorship.

C. Manuscripts

It is very rare for a local chronicle to survive in a large number of medieval manuscripts. The local chronicle was by definition written for a local public, usually the community whose history it contained, and one or two copies were normally deemed sufficient. Thus we have only one copy of the *Inven-*

[10] See above p. 19-20.

[11] Ed. van HOUTS, t. 1, p. lx-lxi, lxv-lxvi, xciii.

[12] Ed. HALPHEN-POUPARDIN, p. xviii-xxvi, xxvii-xlvi.

tio et Miracula sancti Vulfranni from Saint-Wandrille, now Le Havre BM MS 322 (s. xi), and of Emo's *Chronicle of Wittewierum* from Wittewierum, now Groningen UB MS 116 (s. xiii) both of them autograph manuscripts. Only one complete manuscript of Hugh the Chanter's *History of the church of York* survives, now York Minster Library MS L2/1, but this is a beautifully executed copy from the fourteenth century. In these three cases, the manuscripts have survived in or near the places where they were first written. Of Alcuin's poem on York three early manuscripts survive. They originate from the area of Reims, rather than from York, and Godman has suggested that that is where the poem was first written. Their existence suggests that the French liked it as a piece of literature rather than as a local chronicle[13].

Manuscripts of town chronicles were commonly preserved in the towns they dealt with. Caffaro's *Chronicle* and its continuations to 1297 survive in a splendid 13th-century manuscript from Genoa, now Paris BN MS Lat. 10136, which was kept for centuries at the city's archives. A handful of later copies all derive from this one[14]. Dandolo's *Chronicle of Venice* has survived in many more manuscripts because the work was copied by many individual citizens who used it as a starting point for their own private family histories[15]. In Alsace, Jakob Twinger's vernacular chronicle of Strassbourg served very much as a regional chronicle judging by the fact that fifty manuscripts originated from the province rather than from the town[16]. Some of the most beautifully executed town chronicles come from Switserland. I have already mentioned Diebold Schilling's lavishly illustrated work. His *Berner Chronik*, now Berne Burgerbibliothek MS h.h.I. 1-3, was a show piece used by the town council to display their civic pride[17].

Manuscripts of dynastic chronicles are particularly widespread. Such a chronicle was of interest throughout the territory held or controlled by the family and in neighbouring provinces too. An example of a chronicle which was exceptionally widely copied is the *gesta* of the dukes of Normandy. The forty-eight surviving manuscripts originated from Normandy, England, Flanders, the Ile-de-France, Anjou and the Loire valley. A more typical example is the *gesta* of the counts of

[13] Ed. GODMAN, p. cxiii-cxxix.

[14] Ed. BELGRANO, t. 1, p. xxii-xxxvi.

[15] COCHRANE, *Historians*, p. 62-3.

[16] *CDS*, t. 8, p. 199-224. In his preface (t. 8, p. 231) he says that he will write about: 'neuhaftigen dingen die zü Strosburg und zü Elsass und in den Landen do bi geschehen sind.'

[17] *Diebold Schilling, Berner Chronik*, ed. H. BLOESCH, P. HILBER, Bern, 1943-5, 4 vol. (a facsimile of the Bern manuscript).

Anjou of which thirteen, mostly Anjevin, manuscripts survive[18]. The lack of information about private libraries of aristocratic families in the early and High Middle Ages hinders any assessment of the extent that copies of their dynastic chronicles circulated outside monasteries or churches.

D. CONTEXT

The place of a chronicle within a larger collection of manuscripts in a single volume can also offer us a glimpse about the purpose for which it was kept and referred to - usually to check precedents, no doubt, and in cases of litigation. Chronicles of monasteries and churches were normally kept together with related local material, like saints' lives, letters or commemoration lists, annals and charters; the combination with cartularies was especially common. Town chronicles were frequently bound up with registers of minutes, law books, or other documents of the town's administration. Many of them served, as I pointed out above, as so-called feud books recording military matters, like recruitment of soldiers, their payment, the number of casualties in war and so forth[19]. Dynastic and regional chronicles were often copied in manuscripts together with similar texts concerning other families and regions. for example, the *Gesta Normannorum Ducum* served as a regional chronicle within France and there it was copied alongside material from Saint-Denis and Fleury in volumes devoted to French history. In England, however, it provided a base for post-conquest histories because it set out the Norman ancestry of William the Conqueror. The context, however, makes it clear that the Norman dukes were given a place in the line of succession of the English kings. After 1066 the *Gesta* accompanies Geoffrey of Monmouth's *Historia Regum Anglorum*, Henry of Huntingdon's *Historia Anglorum* and William of Malmesbury' s *Gesta Regum Anglorum*[20]. Thus the insertion of a chronicle into a larger collection is significant, because it gives us an idea how the contemporary or later public interpreted the text and how it may have functioned once the author had finished it.

18 Ed. HALPHEN-POUPARDIN, p. lxix - lxxxiii.

19 SCHMIDT, *Die deutschen Städtechroniken*, p. 16-18.

20 Van HOUTS, *Gesta Normannorum Ducum*, p. 175-6.

CHAPTER V

INTEREST FOR HISTORY

The most obvious respect in which chronicles are of interest for the modern historian is that they constitute invaluable sources of information about past events. Viewed simply as sources, it goes without saying that they become less reliable the further back they go. Most of the examples referred to in this volume were written by people who lived in and knew about the area described, and they can normally be relied on where they concern events in the chronicler's own lifetime. They are also reliable, in many cases, as records of happenings in the lifetimes of his father and grandfather. But beyond three generations into the author's past they are not to be trusted unless corroborated by independent sources; they should be read with common-sense scepticism and checked wherever possible.

It must always be remembered that local and regional chronicles were written for a contemporary public. Even those chronicles which reveal that they were composed with 'posterity' in mind were addressed in the first place to an audience which knew what everyday medieval life was like; they were not addressed to people as far removed in time as we are today. The modern historian must patiently unravel, therefore, many incidental details which the medieval chronicler took for granted. In trying to do this, one can very easily go wrong, and error is the more likely if one relies on modern historical handbooks rather than on the texts themselves. A conscious effort of imagination is needed to place oneself in the shoes of one's medieval predecessor and to adopt his perspective. One example will suffice to demonstrate this point.

Modern genealogists are notoriously sceptical about the value of medieval genealogies especially when to be found in dynastic chronicles. Robert of Torigni (d. 1186) included many genealogies of important local families in his version of the *Gesta Normannorum Ducum* and in his *World chronicle* and these have often been rejected as fanciful compilations, put together in order to flatter his contemporaries, and not historically accurate. Charter evidence, however, has shown that Robert is more often right than wrong. For example, he refers to Godehilde de Tosny as daughter of Ralph II of Tosny and wife of Robert of Neubourg and one eminent historian has dismissed this statement on the grounds that Ralph II died in 1102 and could not possibly have have been the father of someone who lived so much later. However, Robert of Torigni knew as Ralph II the man we know as Ralph III; the Ralph we know as Ralph I had died in 1024 and Robert of Torigni, writing more than a century later, did not count him. Another example of Robert's alleged inaccuracy is the occurrence in one of his genealogies of the toponym Bacqueville. Were this to mean Bacqueville[-sur-Andelle] it could not be correct, but Robert was thinking of Bacqueville-en-Caux instead[1].

Local and regional chronicles are primary sources, then, reliable if read with care and imagination, which tell us what happened in a particular community over a number of years. They provide a chronological framework into which information from other sources - from other documents, from inscriptions or from archeological excavations - may be inserted. They provide genealogical information. They provide descriptions of religious ceremonies or pagan practises, which tell us much more about the customs prevalent in specific locations at specific periods than we can learn from canon law collections. And they provide factual information which is found nowhere else. Some chronicles, for example, contain unique accounts of natural disasters - of epidemics, floods or fires. Some record, usually as evidence of a town's prosperity, prices of food, wool or other industrial products.

Besides such information of a factual kind, chronicles contain useful material of a less objective nature. The chronicler may shed light on the prejudices and convictions of his own time, for example, by revealing his own opinions. Sometimes he does this explicitly, but more often not. His aim was normally to make sense of his past and present by linking together the causes and effects of people's actions, and his own opinions are often apparent from the links which he claims to establish. In a basic set of local annals the links may be tenuous and difficult to discern[2]. In more sophisticated texts like the *gesta principum*, however, where events are narrated within a carefully ordered structure, the causality of the chronicler's argument is firmly established.

[1] E.M.C. van HOUTS, *Robert of Torigni as genealogist*, in *Studies in medieval history presented to R. Allen BROWN*, ed. C. HARPER-BILL, C. HOLDSWORTH and J. NELSON, Woodbridge, 1989, p. 215-33.

[2] More research is needed on the problem of causality and language in medieval chronicles. A good example is C. CLARK, *The narrative mode of the Anglo-Saxon Chronicle before the Norman Conquest*, in *England before the conquest: Studies in primary sources presented to Dorothy WHITELOCK*, ed. P. CLEMOES and K. HUGUES, Cambridge, 1971, p. 215-35.

The chronicles are also important sources, as we have seen, for the commemoration of ancestors. In monasteries, churches, noble courts and towns the chronicles illustrate the importance people attached to property. To be able to establish one's title to property it was essential to be able to trace one's line of descent. So a family's acestors had to be recorded. Records also enabled people to pray for their ancestors by name. By doing this, they hoped not only to ensure eternal salvation for the souls of these ancestors but also to set an example which their descendants would in due course follow. They sought to establish an uninterrupted succession of prayers from one generation to the next. I have already referred to the important role women had in this respect. They in particular were expected to keep the family traditions alive and pass them on to their children and grandchildren. This task may explain the important role women played as preservers of the past as dedicatees of historical works, patrons of chroniclers or indeed as chroniclers themselves. The local and regional chronicles are significant sources for our knowledge of the role of women in society.

Chroniclers and their patrons were inevitably influenced by political considerations, and most chronicles are to be viewed as being, at least in some degree, instruments of political propaganda, written to justify particular courses of action. They help us to understand, therefore, how power and authority were established, challenged and denied. The power struggles recorded in local chronicles are naturally local in scale, involving participants who were closely acquainted with one another. A local monastic chronicle, for example, may relate how the monks disputed with their local secular lord or their bishop concerning privileges associated with rights or lands in their neighbourhood. But chronicles of wider geographical scope deal with dissension on a larger scale. In the dynastic chronicles and *gesta principum* , concerned as they are with the succession in office of members of one family or with legitimisation of a change of dynasty, the struggle for power between great lords and lesser ones is a recurrent theme. The regional chronicles chart the process of emancipation from feelings of allegiance to a family, dynasty or institution to feelings of allegiance to a region, and the consequent growth of nationalism in the Middle Ages. The town chronicles chart in the same way the growth of civic pride and political independance. Whereas charters and other legal documents highlight single cases, chronicles follow series of disputes and settlements over long periods of time. They provide us with a long term rather than a short term view of how society responded to political tensions.

Once a chronicle in manuscript was handed over to scribes for copying the original author lost control of it, and some chronicles were extensively altered by later generations for political purposes which the author could not have contemplated. William of Jumièges would have been horrified had he known how Orderic Vitalis, half English by birth, was to alter his account of the Norman conquest of England forty years later. In mid-fifteenth century Bavaria there was a dispute between Duke Louis the Rich of Bavaria-Landshut and Count Albert Achilles of Hohenzollern, as to which had the right to hold the *Landsgericht* in Nuremberg. Duke Louis claimed precedence on the basis of one myth and Count Albert claimed precedence on the basis of another. Chronicles in support of each side were written and used as evidence[3].

Chronicles from the early Middle Ages were invariably copied by members of the clergy, monks or nuns and preserved in monastic or church libraries. Most of them were written by them as well, or, occasionally by lay men. Collectively they form an impressive testament to the significance of monasteries and churches as repositories of historical knowledge. In the later Middle Ages, however, one may detect a growth in the importance of secular archives. It was matched by the increasing use of the vernacular languages in place of Latin to suit the demands of lay aristocrats and lay townspeople.

Finally, it is worth stressing that information of value to the modern historian is to be found in the alterations, interlinear additions, corrections and erasures which are revealed by careful study of the surviving manuscripts of chronicles. The autograph manuscripts are particularly instructive; from them we can see how the author changed his mind over a period of years, sometimes decades, as his work progressed. But later copies deserve study too. Most of them contain illuminating annotations of one sort or another which give us some insight into how, as time passed, the attitudes of readers changed. Thus it is vital for historians who are seriously interested in chronicles to work with modern text editions, which record all annotations fully.

[3] J.M. MOEGLIN, *L'utilisation de l'histoire comme instrument de légitimation: une controverse historique entre Wittelsbach et Hohenzollern en 1459-60*, in *L'historiographie médiévale en Europe*, ed. J.P. GENET, Paris, 1991, p. 217-31 and *Dynastische Bewusstsein und Geschichtsschreibung. Zum Selbstverständnis der Wittelsbacher, Habsburger und Hohenzollern im Spätmittelalter*, in *Historische Zeitschrift*, 256 (1993), p. 593-635.

Déja paru:

1 : L. Genicot, *Introduction* / 1972 / 36 p. 2-503-36001-7
2 : G. Fransen, *Les décrétales et les collections de décrétales* / 1972 / 48 p. + 7 p. mise à jour 2-503-36003-3
3 : L. Genicot, *Les actes publics* / 1972 / 52 p. + 13 p. mise à jour 2-503-36003-3
4 : † N. Huyghebaert, *Les documents nécrologiques* / 1972 / 76 p. + 15 p. mise à jour par J.-L. Lemaitre 2-503-36004-1
5 : R. Noël, *Les dépôts de pollens fossiles* / 1972 / 96 P. + diagr. H.T. + 18 p. mise à jour 2-503-36005-x
6 : Ph. Godding, *La jurisprudence* / 1973 / 44 p. 2-503-36006-8
7 : A.Matthys, *La céramique* / 1973 / 72 p. 2-503-36007-6
8 : M. Smeyers, *La miniature* / 1974 / 124 p. + 32 p. mise à jour 2-503-36008-4
9 : A. Sempoux, *La nouvelle* / 1973 / 36 p. + 8 p. mise à jour 2-503-36009-2
10 : G. Fransen, *Les collections canoniques* / 1973 / 56 p. + 10 p. m:ise à jour 2-503-36010-6
11 : O. Pontral, *Les status synodaux* / 1975 / 100 p. 2-503-36011-4
12 : † J.-Ch. Payen & F. Dieckstra, *Le roman* / 1975 / 160 p. + 8 p. mise à jour 2-503-36012-2
13 : O. Jodogne & † J.-Ch. Payen, *Le fabliau et le lai narratif* / 1975 / 64 p. + 11 p. mise à jour 2-503-36013-O
14 : M. McCormick, *Les annales du haut moyen âge* / 1975 / 56 p. 2-503-36014-9
15 : L. Genicot, *Les généalogies* / 1975 / 44 p. + 12 p. mise à jour 2-503-36015-7
16 : K.H. Krüger, *Die Universalchroniken* / 1976 / 64 p. + 16 p. mise à jour 2-503-36016-5
17 : G. Constable, *Letters and Letter-Collections* / 1976 / 68 p. 2-503-36017-3
18 : M.-A. Arnould, *Les relevés de feux* / 1976 / 98 p. + 13 p. mise à jour 2-503-36018-1
19 : G. Despy, *Les tarifs de tonlieux* / 1976 / 48 p. 2-503-36019-x
20 : M. Pastoureau, *Les armoiries* / 1976 / 84 p. + 14 p. mise à jour 2-503-36020-3
21 : Ph. Grierson, *Les monnaies* / 1977 / 52 p. 2-503-36021-1
22 : L. Genicot, *La loi* / 1977 / 56 p. + 10 mise à jour 2-503-36022-x
23 : N. Coulet, *Les visites pastorales* / 1977 / 88 p. + 25 p. mise à jour 2-503-36023-8
24-25 : G. Philippart, *Les légendiers et autres manuscrits hagiographiques* / 1977 / 140 p. + 42 p. mise à jour 2-503-36024-6
26 : J. Dubois, *Les martyrologes du moyen âge latin* / 1978 / 90 p. + 9 p. mise à jour 2-503-36026-2
27 : † C. Vogel, *Les "libri paenitentiales"* / 1978 / 116 p. + 49 p. mise à jour 2-503-36027-2
28 : R. Fossier, *Les polyptiques et censiers* / 1978 / 72 p. 2-503-36028-9
29 : L.-F. Genicot, *L'architecture. Considérations générales* / 1978 / 88 p. 2-503-36029-7
30 : C. Thiry, *La plainte funèbre* / 1978 / 92 p. + 3 p. mise à jour 2-503-36030-0

31 : A. Derolez, *Les catalogues de bibliothèques* / 1979 / 72 p. 2-503-36031-9

32 : R. Halleux, *Les textes alchimiques* / 1979 / 156 p. 2-503-36032-7

33 : M. Heinzelmann, *Translationsberichte und andere Quellen des Reliquienkultes* / 1979 / 128 p. 2-503-36033-5

34 : C. Gaier, *Les armes* / 1979 / 96 p. + 10 p. mise à jour 2-503-36034-3

35 : R. Favreau, *Les inscriptions médiévales* / 1979 / 128 p. + 7 p. mise à jour 2-503-36035-1

36 : M. Pastoureau, *Les sceaux* / 1981 / 80 p. 2-503-36036-X

37 : M. Sot, *"Gesta episcoporum, gesta abbatum"* / 1981 / 60 p. + 3 p. mise à jour 2-503-36037-8

38 : J. Richard, *Les récits de voyages et de pèlerinages* / 1981 / 88 p. + 6 p. mise à jour 2-503-36038-6

39 : E. Poulle, *Les sources astronomiques: textes, tables, instruments* / 1981 / 88 p. 2-503-36039-4

40 : C. Bremond, J. Le Goff, J.-C. Schmitt, *L' "exemplum"* / 1982 / 168 p. 2-503-36040-8

41 : J. Gilissen, *La coutume* / 1982 / 122 p. 2-503-36041-6

42 : M. Pastoureau, *Jetons, méreaux et médailles* / 1985 / 48 p. 2-503-36042-4

43 : P. Brommer, *"Capitula episcoporum". Die bischöflichen Kapitularien des 9. und 10. Jahrhunderts* / 1985 / 71 p. 2-503-36044-0

44-45 : B.C. Bazàn, J.F. Wippel, G. Fransen & D. Jacquart, *Les questions disputées et les questions quodlibétiques dans les Facultés de Théologie, de Droit et de Médecine* / 1985 / 317 p. 2-503-36045-9

46 : A. de Vogüé, *Les Règles monastiques anciennes (400-700)* / 1985 / 62 p. 2-503-36046-7

47 : M. Madou, *Le costume civil* / 1986 / 67 p. 2-503-36047-5

48 : G. van Dievoet, *Les coutumiers, les styles, les formulaires et les "artes notariae"* / 1986 / 86 p. 2-503-36048-3

49 : R. Boyer, D. Bushinger, A. Crepin, J. Flori, J.-M. Paquette, F. Suard, M. Tyssens, J. Victorio, sous la direction de J. Victorio avec la collaboration de J.-C. Payen (†), *L'épopée* / 1987 / 252 p. 2-503-36049-1

50 : A. Graboïs, *Les sources hébraïques médiévales. Volume I: Chroniques, Lettres et "Responsa"* / 1987 / 96 p. 2-503-36050-5

51 : A.-D. von den Brincken, *Kartographische Quellen. Welt-, See- und Regionalkarten* / 1988 / 117 p. + 9 ill. 2-503-36051-3

52 : M. Huglo, *Les livres de chant liturgique* / 1988 / 141 p. 2-503-36052-1

53 : A.-V. Munaut, *Les cernes de croissance des arbes (La dendrochronologie)* / 1988 / 51 p. 2-503-36053-x

54 : D.P. Blok, *Ortsnamen* / 1988 / 51 p. 2-503-36054-8

55 : J. Szövérffy, *Latin Hymns* / 1989 / 141 p. 2-503-36055-6

56 : A.-G. Martimort, *Les "ordines", les ordinaires et les cérémoniaux* / 1991 / 123 p. 2-503-36056-4

57 : P. Dinzelbacher, *Revelationes* / 1991 / 108 p. 2-503-36057-2

58 : J.O. Ward, *Ciceronian Rhetoric in Treatise, Scholion and Commentary* / 1995 / 376 p. 2-503-36058-0

59 : D. Kelly, *The Arts of Poetry and Prose* / 1991 / 180 p. 2-503-36059-9

60 : M. Camargo, *"Ars dictaminis", "ars dictandi"* / 1991 / 59 p. 2-503-36060-2

61 : M.G. Briscoe and B.H. Jaye, *"Artes praedicandi" and "Artes orandi"* / 1992 / 120 p. 2-503-36061-0

62 : R. Boyer, *La poésie scaldique* / 1992 / 92 p. 2-503-36062-9

63 : L. Fowler-Margerl, *"Ordines iudiciara" and "Libelli de ordine iudiciorum"* / 1994 / 131 p. 2-503-36063-7

64 : A.G. Martimort, *Les lectures liturgiques et leurs livres* / 1992 / 105 p. 2-503-36064-5

L. Genicot, *Table des Fascicules* 1-50 – *Table of fascicles* 1-50 – *Register der Faszikel* 1-50 / 1992 / 113 p. 2-503-50261-x

65 : J. Paquet, *Les matricules universitaires* / 1992 / 152 p. 2-503-36065-3

66 : A Graboïs, *Les sources hébraïques médiévales.* Volume II: *Les commentaires exégétiques* / 1993 / 65 p. 2-503-36066-1

67 : F. Joubert, *La tapisserie* / 1993 / 56 p. 2-503-36067-x

68 : R. Newhauser, *The treatise on vices and virtues in Latins and the Vernacular* / 1993 / 210 p. 2-503-36068-8

69 : J. Agrimi et C. Crisciani, *Les "consilia "médicaux* / 1994 / 108 p. 2-503-36069-6

70 : M. Metzger, *Les sacramentaires* / 1994 / 140 p. 2-503-36070-x

71 : M. Richter, *Oral Tradition in the early middle Ages* / 1994 / 79 p. 2-503-36071-8

72 : J. Stiennon, *L'écriture* / 1995 / 128 p. + 5 ill. 2-503-36072-6

73 : A. Verhulst, *Le paysage rural: les structures parcellaires de l'Europe du Nord-Ouest* / 1995 / 85 p. + 24 ill. 2-503-36073-4

74 : E.M.C. Van Houts , *Local and regional Chronicles.* / 1995 / 62 p. 2-503-36074-2

Imprimé par Brepols S.A. - Turnhout (Belgique)
Printed in Belgium
D/1995/0095/34
ISBN 2-503-36000-9
ISBN 2-503-36074-2